Frank J. Fabozzi, CFA
Yale School of Management

Sergio M. Focardi
EDHEC Business School

Caroline Jonas
The Intertek Group

Investment Management after the Global Financial Crisis

RESEARCH FOUNDATION
OF CFA INSTITUTE

Statement of Purpose

The Research Foundation of CFA Institute is a not-for-profit organization established to promote the development and dissemination of relevant research for investment practitioners worldwide.

ISBN 978-1-934667-32-3

1 October 2010

Biographies

Frank J. Fabozzi, CFA, is professor of finance and Becton Fellow in the Yale School of Management and editor of the *Journal of Portfolio Management*. Prior to joining the Yale faculty, Professor Fabozzi was a visiting professor of finance in the Sloan School of Management at Massachusetts Institute of Technology. He is a fellow of the International Center for Finance at Yale University, is on the advisory council for the Department of Operations Research and Financial Engineering at Princeton University, and is an affiliated professor at the Institute of Statistics, Econometrics and Mathematical Finance at the University of Karlsruhe in Germany. Professor Fabozzi has authored and edited numerous books about finance. In 2002, he was inducted into the Fixed Income Analysts Society's Hall of Fame, and he is the recipient of the 2007 C. Stewart Sheppard Award from CFA Institute. Professor Fabozzi holds a doctorate in economics from the City University of New York.

Sergio M. Focardi is a professor of finance at EDHEC Business School, Nice, France, and a founding partner of The Intertek Group. Professor Focardi is on the editorial board of the *Journal of Portfolio Management* and has co-authored numerous articles and books, including the Research Foundation of CFA Institute monograph *Trends in Quantitative Finance* and *Challenges in Quantitative Equity Management* as well as the award-winning books *Financial Modeling of the Equity Market: CAPM to Cointegration* and *The Mathematics of Financial Modeling and Investment Management*. Most recently, Professor Focardi co-authored *Financial Econometrics: From Basics to Advanced Modeling Techniques* and *Robust Portfolio Optimization and Management*. Professor Focardi holds a degree in electronic engineering from the University of Genoa, Italy, and a PhD in mathematical finance from the University of Karlsruhe, Germany.

Caroline Jonas is a founding partner of The Intertek Group, where she is responsible for research projects. She is a co-author of various reports and articles on finance and technology and co-author of the 2008 Research Foundation of CFA Institute monograph *Challenges in Quantitative Equity Management*. Ms. Jonas holds a BA from the University of Illinois at Urbana–Champaign.

Contents

CFA Institute
CE Qualified Activity

This publication qualifies for 5 CE credits under the guidelines of the CFA Institute Continuing Education Program.

Foreword

Only rarely do we in the investment management profession have the pleasure—or pain—of seeing a major secular change in our own line of work unfold before our eyes. In the working lifetimes of most readers of this book, many social, technological, and business changes have taken place—in particular, the emergence of the computer as the primary work tool and the internet as the principal means of communication. But these are changes in the infrastructure of our work, not in the essence of it. The 40 years prior to the crash of 2007–2009 have seen only two truly major changes in what economists call the "industrial organization" of the investment profession: (1) in the 1970s and 1980s, the creation of a critical mass of independent investment management firms and the migration of assets from banks and insurance companies to these new institutions and (2) in the 1990s and 2000s, the emergence of alternative investments as a serious challenge to traditional investment managers and their risk-controlled, benchmark-sensitive portfolios. We may be on the verge of a third such change in response to the global financial crisis and market crash of 2007–2009.[1]

What is the nature of the changes that have yet to unfold? We can speculate:

- New regulations will limit leverage in an attempt to avoid the "necessity" of further bailouts; the role of moral hazard and principal–agent conflicts in investing and in corporate management will come to the forefront.

- The desire to avoid paying alpha fees for beta performance will lead investors increasingly to allocate funds to low-fee index strategies and to high-fee, but potentially high-returning, hedge funds. Traditional active management may be in trouble.

- The shift in retirement finance from defined-benefit (DB) pensions to defined-contribution (DC) savings plans, now in its third decade, will likely result in almost everyone being covered by DC plans. Even public plans, the last bastion of DB plans, are facing a funding crisis on a scale not contemplated before the economic crisis, which affected tax revenues very negatively. (Tax revenues are hypersensitive to economic activity.) This situation is not good. It has been said, and it is only a modest exaggeration, that the worst DB plan is a better guarantor of the retirement security of the mass of participants than the best DC plan. DC plans, however, will improve greatly through the use of efficient portfolios, cost-saving annuities, and other "innovations" (conceptually more than half a century old but still in need of being implemented).

---

[1]By focusing on industrial organization, we can overlook (for the sake of the present argument) such wonders as the emergence of derivatives and of index funds. These are changes in technology, which may or may not lead to changes in industrial organization.

- In a related trend, the investment management profession will pay more attention to the individual investor, as it did in our grandfathers' day.
- A new type of financial institution—the sovereign wealth fund—will continue to emerge and thrive.
- Retail acceptance of alternative investments will broaden, and new technologies will be developed to broaden the reach of these investments.

Change is always interesting to observe, but it is not always good. Although transaction costs have fallen dramatically, investment management fees are probably the highest they have ever been. As a result, because of the zero-sum arithmetic of active management, after-fee performance relative to benchmarks must be the *lowest* it has ever been! Some investment managers may be worth these fees and then some, but we cannot all be worth such high average fees.

But are we on the verge of a change in investment institutions that brings fees down to an economically justifiable level? I do not see it happening quickly, and the survey evidence presented in this timely monograph by veteran Research Foundation of CFA Institute writers Frank Fabozzi, CFA, Sergio Focardi, and Caroline Jonas suggests that fees are not likely to fall as quickly as customers might like. There are, however, "green shoots" that suggest the direction of change is the right one. For example, a 2 and 20 hedge fund mandate is now a rarity.

Among the many changes documented by these authors, who with this volume are presenting their third survey-based study of investment management trends, perhaps the most welcome is that asset allocation is back on top. Good—because that is where it belongs. A sign of the times is that the prestigious Institute for Quantitative Research in Finance (the Q-Group) is producing a seminar called "No Alpha Now? So Let's Work on Beta." Yes, let's do that and build the building instead of just the ornamentations.

The first two Research Foundation monographs written by these authors (with some personnel changes among the authors) studied trends in quantitative finance. This book substantially expands the authors' territory to cover the whole investment management industry, not just that part of it that specializes in quantitative methods and approaches. They ask where the most profound changes are likely to be as the industry regroups from the disasters of recent years and moves forward into the future. We are exceptionally pleased to present it.

Laurence B. Siegel
Research Director
Research Foundation of CFA Institute

Preface

From mid-2007 through the first quarter of 2009, financial markets were shaken by a series of shocks. The first was the shock in the summer of 2007 in which liquidity dried up and the subprime mortgage crisis began. Then, following the collapse of Lehman Brothers in September 2008, the financial markets began a slide that caused major indices, such as the S&P 500 Index and the MSCI Index, to lose more than half their value compared with their highs in 2007. By the end of the first quarter of 2009, most investors had suffered serious losses and asset management firms were in survival mode.

With this scenario in mind, the Research Foundation of CFA Institute commissioned the authors to research how the financial crisis affected and will continue to affect investment management decisions and processes as well as the investment management industry itself. This monograph is the result. It is based on a review of the literature and on conversations with industry players, industry observers, executive recruiters, and academics. Most interviews were conducted in the second half of 2009, and they reflect opinions expressed at that time. Academics contributed their evaluations in early 2010. In total, in-depth interviews were conducted with 68 people from the following groups:

- 17 institutional investors with a total of €570 billion in investable assets,
- 15 investment consultants and private wealth advisers with around €5 trillion in assets under advisory,
- 15 asset and wealth managers with around €4.5 trillion assets under management,
- 6 industry observers,
- 6 executive recruiters, and
- 9 academics.

Among institutional investors, we talked to managing directors or chief investment officers at funds in Austria (1), Belgium (1), Great Britain (4), the Netherlands (4), Sweden (2), Canada (1), and the United States (4). The funds had investable assets between €1 billion and more than €200 billion (9 of the 17 had investable assets between €18 billion and €35 billion) and included 10 corporate funds, 3 public-sector funds, 2 industrywide funds, and 2 buffer funds.

Among investment consultants (12) and private wealth advisers (3), we talked to heads of investment consulting at firms in Germany (2), Great Britain (4), the Netherlands (2), Switzerland (2), and the United States (5). Assets under advisory ranged from €2 billion to US$2 trillion.

Among asset managers, we talked to the business heads or chief investment officers at firms in Austria (1), France (2), Great Britain (3), Luxembourg (1), Switzerland (3), and the United States (5). Assets under management at these firms ranged from €9 billion to more than €1 trillion.

One source said, "For everyone in asset management—managers, consultants, and institutional investors—it is vital to do a 'lessons learned' exercise. The industry failed to do so when the internet bubble burst in 2000; everyone said that it was the investment banks, brushed it off, and moved on. This time we need to do a lessons learned exercise at every level; we need to understand the 10 things that we need to do differently." The authors hope that this book will contribute to the exercise.

Acknowledgements

The authors wish to thank all those who contributed to this book by sharing their experience and their views. This includes a sincere thank you to institutional investors, investment consultants, asset managers, and industry observers to whom we promised anonymity, as well as to the executive recruitment agencies Godliman Partners (London), Indigo Headhunters (Frankfurt, Germany), Johnson Associates (New York), RAH Partners (London), and Russell Reynolds Associates (New York and London). A special thanks to the following contributors from academia who accepted the challenge to articulate their views on lessons learned from the market crash of 2008–2009 and, more generally, on the implications for the theory and practice of investment management: Noël Amenc (professor of finance, EDHEC Business School, and the director of EDHEC-Risk Institute), Jonathan B. Berk (A.P. Giannini Professor of Finance, Graduate School of Business, Stanford University), John Finnerty (professor and director of the MS in quantitative finance program, Fordham University), Roger Ibbotson (professor of finance, Yale School of Management), Lionel Martellini (professor of finance, EDHEC Business School, and scientific director of EDHEC-Risk Institute), Stephen Schaefer (professor of finance, London Business School), Allan Timmermann (Atkinson/Epstein Endowed Chair and professor of finance, Rady School of Management, University of California, San Diego), Guofu Zhou (Frederick Bierman and James E. Spears Professor of Finance, Olin Business School, Washington University), and Yu Zhu (professor of finance, China Europe International Business School).

The authors are also grateful to the Research Foundation of CFA Institute for funding this project and to its research director, Laurence B. Siegel, for his encouragement and assistance.

1. Introduction

Financial markets were shaken by a series of shocks from mid-2007 through the first quarter of 2009. When equity markets bottomed out in March 2009, major indices, such as the S&P 500 Index and the MSCI Index, had lost more than half of their value compared with their highs of 2007, investors had suffered serious losses, and many asset management firms were in survival mode while others had gone out of business.

The Research Foundation of CFA Institute asked the authors to research how investors, investment consultants, and asset managers evaluated the impact of the crisis on investment management decision making, strategies, and products, as well as on the investment management industry itself. The authors gathered their information from sources in North America and western Europe (for details, see the Preface).

The results are presented in subsequent chapters and can be summarized as follows:

- *Chapter 2, Asset Allocation Revisited.* The recent market turmoil clearly reestablished the key role of asset allocation in generating returns and protecting the downside. The events of 2007–2009 highlighted the need for a top-down approach in which macroeconomics plays a much bigger role than it has in recent times. Given the high levels of volatility in this period, which are expected to continue, asset allocation is also becoming more dynamic, even though asset managers and pension fund sponsors may not be embracing tactical asset allocation and global dynamic asset allocation. The difficult task of *timing* asset allocation decisions will play a big role in explaining returns.

  Investors are turning to greater diversification in asset classes to protect assets from market movements and generate higher returns. The investable universe that once centered around two asset classes—equities and bonds—has been expanded to include new strategies and asset classes, including real estate, hedge funds, private equity, currencies, commodities, natural resources (e.g., forests and agricultural land), infrastructure, and intangibles (e.g., intellectual property rights). The percentage of alternatives in the aggregate asset allocation of the pension funds in the seven countries with the largest pensions markets was estimated to be more than 16 percent by year-end 2008.[2] Not much history exists, however, on the performance of many of these alternative asset classes.

---

[2]In decreasing order of size, these countries are the United States, Japan, the United Kingdom, the Netherlands, Canada, Australia, and Switzerland.

In this context, such concepts as the core–satellite approach and benchmarking are losing relevance. With asset allocation reestablished as the most important factor explaining returns, asset allocation products are expected to have strong growth. Investment products with an element of active asset allocation are now being engineered for defined-contribution plan members and retail investors. Lifestyle funds are one example.

- *Chapter 3, Risk Management Revisited.* Recent market turmoil has led investors to reduce their exposure to market risk. The failure to foresee the crash was largely attributed to a focus on returns rather than on risk—something investors will likely be changing. In addition to paying more attention to market risk in their portfolios, investors will likely be paying more attention to liquidity risk, counterparty risk, systemic risk, and the effects of leverage.

  The risk measure called value at risk (VaR), which is widely used by market participants, has well-known limitations. Rather than blame this measure for its failure to identify the possibility of a financial crisis, however, one must instead blame the way that risk measures were (or were not) used by investors, their advisers, and asset managers. To gain a better appreciation of risk, such methodologies as Monte Carlo simulations, stress testing, conditional VaR, and extreme value theory are being adopted.

  Innovative products, such as those introduced by investment banks, are blamed for having added an element of risk. Innovative products call not only for special methodologies for measuring their risk but also for a greater understanding of the products one is investing in. The size of return expectations for specific products will have to be better aligned with the overall ability of markets and the economy to generate returns.

- *Chapter 4, Cutting Management Fees and Other Costs.* Investors who saw their assets shrink as major indices lost around half of their value in the crash of 2008–2009 are taking a hard look at management fees and other costs. Institutional investors are responding by renegotiating fees (especially, but not only, in the alternatives arena), investing more assets in index funds, bringing management (increasingly) in-house including, for the larger funds, setting up in-house teams to manage alternative investments, and pooling assets to wring out layers of intermediaries.

  As for high-net-worth individuals, the issue of hidden fees in private-bank commissions and fund-of-funds products has come to the forefront as investors look at fee statements in the wake of losses. The affluent are moving toward simpler, more transparent products, such as exchange-traded funds (ETFs), and toward banks that offer more competitive fees and more competitive products. Retail investors are also trying to reduce management fees by putting their investable assets into low-cost funds—a trend already underway for a number of years in some markets.

- *Chapter 5, Moving toward a Redistribution of Roles?* A redistribution of roles among investors, consultants, and asset and wealth managers has accelerated as investors, still dealing with recent losses, seek ways to protect their invested assets. Large institutional investors are increasingly bringing asset allocation and asset management in-house, and the largest are building platforms to service smaller funds. Consultants are moving into "implemented" or fiduciary management in an attempt to boost revenues that slumped as the value of assets under management fell and firms sought to control costs. (A consulting relationship that is reconfigured to include the performance of actual asset management services by the consultant is referred to as "implemented.")

  Asset managers are offering asset allocation advice, both in response to investor demand and to provide value above that added in the manager's asset-class mandate. Such an enhanced relationship is important in periods when performance is down. Asset managers are also making inroads with asset allocation in the defined-contribution (DC) pension arena, offering "all-weather" portfolios for DC plan members as plan sponsors seek to give some sort of downside protection to plan members who became shell-shocked as the value of their pension assets fell.

  Investment banks will continue to play an important role in assisting corporate pension plans, providing hedging of liabilities with interest rate derivatives and perhaps, more generally, providing swap-based ETFs. But reputations dented by the events of 2007–2009 and the need to increase their capital base after recent large losses will limit the ability of investment banks to enlarge their role in the pension market. Insurers, however, are expected to play a bigger role as small pension funds outsource the management of their assets, governments try to push down the cost of management, and retiring Baby Boomers demand principal-protection and risk-mitigation products.

- *Chapter 6, Ethical Dimension.* In the wake of the Bernie Madoff and Galleon scandals, consultants and investors are stepping up their due diligence, especially in alternative investments. Larger consultancies are building up their research teams. Institutional investors—burned by hot money in hedge funds—are taking a closer look not only at who is managing the money and how they are managing it but also at who the co-investors are.

  As for the ethics of an investment itself, continental European funds are looking more closely at what activities are behind the profits of the companies in their portfolios; investors in English-speaking countries are focusing more closely on governance and other ethical issues that affect the value of a company.

- *Chapter 7, Challenges.* After the market crash of 2008, the biggest challenge confronting everyone in the asset management industry is to regain the trust of the investor. This effort will require more transparency, more communication with investors (especially about risk), and better management of expectations than is currently done by the asset management industry, as well as some help from financial markets.

Pension funds face the special challenge of paying the pension promise in what many investors expect to be a highly uncertain, low-interest-rate, low-return environment. Such investors will be trying to decrease costs, move more assets to in-house management wherever possible, increase returns with greater diversification and more opportunistic active asset allocation, and at the same time, pay more attention to the macro environment.

Consultants will have to add value as investment strategies pursued by institutional investors become more complex. This trend will require consultants to bolster competencies in risk budgeting, asset allocation, and new asset classes. Some will also be enlarging their service offerings to include, for example, fiduciary management. To address the problem of falling revenues as a result of both recent events and longer-term trends, consultants are also merging or considering alliances with asset managers or institutional investors.

Asset managers will have to redefine their offering, aligning promises with their ability to deliver. They will likely play a bigger role in asset allocation—advising institutional investors and engineering products for retail investors—and in risk and liquidity management. As investors move their assets increasingly into index funds on the one side and alternatives on the other, the industry is expected to restructure, with a few large firms offering a comprehensive set of products, including alternatives and advice, along with a large number of specialized boutiques. As the industry consolidates and the pensions market undergoes "retailization," the industry is moving toward a separation of production and distribution in which revenue sharing will be a major issue.

- *Chapter 8, Employment and Compensation Trends.* Personnel search mandates in the asset and wealth management industry were down 20–55 percent in 2009 compared with 2008, although searches picked up as of mid-2009. The drop in overall recruitment mandates was a result of downsizing at large asset management firms as they tried to control costs as assets under management decreased and investors showed a preference for lower-margin products. Headcounts were reduced across the board in sales, marketing, portfolio management, and back office.

Compensation in the industry was down in 2009 compared with 2008, essentially because of a reduction in bonuses (which were down from 20 percent to more than 50 percent), which brought overall compensation down by 20–40 percent. Compensation structures are also being reviewed, with a larger percentage of compensation being deferred, performance evaluated over several years, and incentives aligned with the long-term performance of the firm.

Positions for which headhunters were recruiting most in 2009 were asset allocation specialists and persons with multi-asset experience and quantitative skills. Demand was strong for risk managers, including counterparty and operational risk managers. Hiring was occurring in fixed income for both managers and analysts, but it was soft in equities and for stock pickers as investors moved assets into index funds. As 2009 progressed and markets recouped losses, there was some demand for asset servicers and gatherers in the institutional arena. In retail, however, shrinking revenues and margins, the decline of the open-architecture model, and consolidation kept recruitment of retail wholesaling staff weak. Asset management boutiques and insurance firms were doing most of the recruiting; large asset management and private equity firms and hedge funds, the least.

- *Chapter 9, Looking Ahead.* The market turmoil of 2008–2009 caught most investors by surprise, although a few economists, notably Minsky (1986) and more recently Reinhart and Rogoff (2008), have provided an analysis of financial crises that suggests, in retrospect, that one was likely to happen. The crisis left many investors questioning modern portfolio theory (MPT), but the academics we interviewed noted that evidence exists that diversification "worked"—that is, losses were mitigated in well-diversified portfolios that included bonds and other nonequity assets. These academics, however, are somewhat skeptical about the contribution made by alternative asset classes to (risk-adjusted) performance. They argue that nonpublic assets should be subject to the same shocks as publicly traded assets, whether or not these shocks are reflected in current market quotes. Academics are equally skeptical about investment managers' ability to successfully time asset allocation decisions if they are not in specific subsets as opposed to broad asset classes.

The crisis heightened awareness of liquidity risk and the need to incorporate liquidity considerations into MPT. Academics underlined the difficulty, however, in hedging liquidity risk based on the lack of data and the likely nonlinear impact of liquidity shocks. Other phenomena that the industry will likely have to consider and model include fat tails (i.e., large events, such as large market movements) and systemic risk. Conditional VaR is one way of measuring risk in the presence of fat tails; in the area of systemic risk, aggregation phenomena are being studied by using such methodologies as the theories of percolation and random networks. As for new risks that result from the complex structured products—risks underlined by industry players—academics cautioned about their use given the asymmetry of experience and lack of competition in the market.

Before beginning our discussion, let's take a brief look at some industry data. According to the research from International Financial Services London (IFSL), US$15.3 trillion in assets were lost in the global fund management industry in 2008.

The report's author, Marko Maslakovic (2009), estimated that assets in the global fund management industry were US$90 trillion at year-end 2008, down 17 percent from the previous year, which reflects the sharp fall in equity markets. Of this amount, US$61.6 trillion, or two-thirds, were estimated to be in traditional investment management assets (US$24 trillion in pension funds, US$18.9 trillion in mutual funds, and US$18.7 trillion in insurance funds); overall, these assets were down 19 percent from the previous year. Among alternative investment management assets, private equity assets were estimated to be US$2.5 trillion at year-end 2008, up 15 percent from the prior year (the author of the report suggested that this increase was the result of strong fund-raising activity); hedge fund assets were US$1.5 trillion, down 30 percent from the prior year; and assets held by high-net-worth individuals (the 8.6 million individuals with more than US$1 million of investable assets) were US$32.8 trillion, down 20 percent from the previous year (see **Figure 1.1**).

In the chapters that follow, we take a closer look at the findings.

Figure 1.1. Assets under Management in the Global Fund Management Industry, 2008

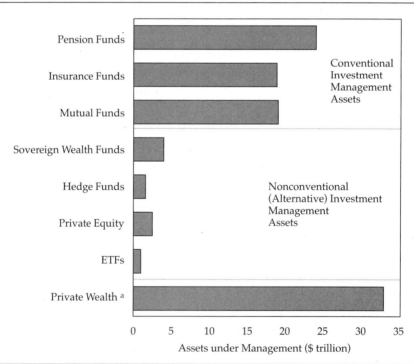

aAround one-third of private wealth is incorporated in conventional investment management.

Source: Based on data from Maslakovic (2009).

©2010 The Research Foundation of CFA Institute

2. Asset Allocation Revisited

The market crash of 2008–2009 highlighted the importance of asset allocation in generating returns for institutional and individual investors alike. Among the sources we interviewed, there is wide agreement that asset allocation is the key factor in explaining returns. As one investment consultant said, referring to investors' reaction to the recent market fall, "One thing that strikes me is the growing client awareness that asset allocation drives everything." However, opinions differ as to how asset allocation decisions should be implemented, in particular, whether asset allocation should be static or dynamic and, if dynamic, just how dynamic. Opinions also differ as regards the merits of the various asset classes considered to be relevant.

New Approaches to Asset Allocation

The classical approach to investment management is a top-down approach that starts with strategic asset allocation (SAA), in which strategic long-term decisions are made about how to allocate assets based on estimates of future returns, risks, and correlations. Traditionally, the two major asset classes have been stocks and bonds. The research group Towers Watson (previously Watson Wyatt Worldwide) estimated (2009) that, at year-end 2008, these two asset classes still represented more than 80 percent of pension assets in the world's seven largest national pension markets. The investment management process then proceeds to implement decisions with a higher level of asset granularity and at a higher time frequency. The last step of the process is portfolio management, in which managers select the individual assets.

The last two decades of the 20th century included three major new developments in asset allocation. First, an element of timing was introduced with global tactical asset allocation (GTAA), in which asset classes are over- or underweighted in response to perceived short- to medium-term opportunities. GTAA is thus performed using short- to medium-term forecasts of asset-class returns, volatility, and correlations. A second element of timing was introduced with global dynamic asset allocation (GDAA), in which asset classes are over- or underweighted to take advantage of long-term opportunities. GDAA works with long-term forecasts, exploiting such price processes as mean reversion. It is typically performed with such techniques as stochastic programming.[3] Both GTAA and GDAA are dynamic insofar as asset allocation decisions are revised in response to changes in market conditions; the fundamental distinction is the time horizon.

---

[3]Stochastic programming is a mathematical optimization technique that reveals the entire development of a stochastic (i.e., random) process. For a discussion of the applicability of stochastic programming to asset allocation, see Ziemba (2003).

The third development, related to GTAA and GDAA, was an expansion of the universe of investable asset classes. Traditional asset classes are stocks, bonds, cash, and real estate. To these, specific equity and other styles are added, especially as they are implemented by hedge funds. To this mix, other asset classes are added, such as currencies, natural resources, precious metals, private equity, infrastructure, and even such intangibles as intellectual property rights. All asset classes except stocks, bonds, and cash are commonly known as alternatives. Towers Watson (2009) estimated that the percentage of alternatives in the aggregate asset allocation of the seven largest national pension markets increased by almost 10 percentage points during 1998–2008, going from 6.8 percent at year-end 1998 to 16.5 percent by year-end 2008 as shown in **Figure 2.1**.

Figure 2.1. Aggregate Asset Allocation from 1998 to 2008 of the Seven Largest National Pension Markets

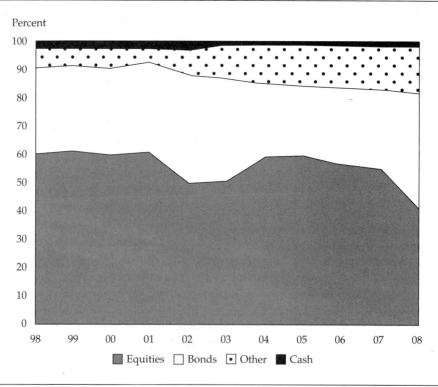

Note: 2007 and 2008 data are estimates.

Source: Based on data from Towers Watson and various secondary sources.

The growth of alternative asset classes started in an investment environment characterized by low interest rates, low expected returns on stocks, and the bursting of the technology, media, and telecommunications bubble in March 2000. Many considered that market crash to be a failure of diversification. To protect investments and deliver returns, many investors argued that greater diversification was required. This approach led some investors to seek returns outside the traditional asset classes and strategies in what some sources referred to as alpha- or return-chasing behavior. The endowments of Yale and Harvard were considered pioneers in this new approach. But the crisis that started in mid-2007 has shown the limitations of this new "endowment model." It has become clear that standard deviation and correlation are not the only dimensions of risk; autocorrelation, which captures the continuation and eventual reversal of trends, must also be considered.

As a consequence, some investors began to adopt an approach that relies more on risk control and insurance than on diversification. A source in Germany commented, "Risk control has grown more important as investors look for a 'guarantee' to limit losses." To better understand the desire for risk controls and guarantees, following is a brief review of the basic principles of risk control.

Risk control can be achieved either through diversification or by subscribing to contracts that offer some level of protection against unforeseeable events. For example, insurance companies pool risks and derivative contracts transfer risk from one entity to another. Both insurance contracts and derivative contracts, however, offer protection only if the counterparties remain solvent. Therefore, it is important to understand the nature of the protection offered.

The entity seeking to control risk must first determine if the need is to control the risk of losses or the risk of fluctuations that might include both gains and losses. Controlling the risk of pure losses is typical of insurance. Insurance works by collecting a payment, called a "premium," that will cover future claims. If potential losses are small, numerous, and uncorrelated, as in the case of auto insurance, the insurer is basically covering a fixed cost. But if the distribution of potential losses is fat tailed, as in the case of earthquakes, the insurer faces the risk of insolvency unless the premiums are adequate and its capital cushion sufficient (see Embrechts, Klüppelberg, and Mikosch 1997).

If the objective is to control the risk of events that involve changes in asset values that are beneficial to some and detrimental to others (e.g., fluctuations in the price of oil or interest rates), derivative contracts might offer protection against one entity's losses that are strongly correlated with another entity's gains. This type of risk control could be considered a natural hedge. The recent crisis showed that because of the complexity of interactions between various derivative contracts, concentrations of risk can occur that make it impossible to honor commitments when an entity seeks to control risk either by setting money aside to cover future losses when no offsetting gain exists or by exchanging gains and losses.

The collapse of Lehman Brothers in September 2008 illustrated just how important counterparty risk is to investors using risk control strategies. The head of a corporate pension fund in the financial services sector remarked, "There is such a thing as counterparty risk. In the past, we used to look at ratings and ask for collateral (proportional to how bad the rating is). We have all learned that collateral and margin calls are very serious business."

Putting Asset Allocation Back on Top

Almost 20 years after Brinson, Singer, and Beebower's (1991) influential paper on the importance of investment policy in explaining, on average, more than 90 percent of the variation of returns over time, along with the period of 2007–2009 in which investors' wealth was affected by fundamental asset allocation decisions, sources were in agreement about the predominant role of asset allocation in protecting investments and delivering returns.

A source in the United States said, "There is now a greater understanding on the part of institutional investors that asset allocation is *the* issue rather than stock picking."

The CIO of a pension fund in northern Europe concurred: "Strategic asset allocation has always been a more important driver of returns than the selection of asset managers that pursue outperformance vis-à-vis a market benchmark."

Two considerations have led most of our sources to this conclusion. First, there is the long-running debate on the ability of asset managers to generate positive alpha (i.e., positive excess returns over the benchmark) that is attributable to skill as opposed to luck. This debate goes beyond saying that the average asset manager cannot produce alpha. Although it is obvious that the "average" manager cannot be above average—that is, produce a positive alpha that signifies above-average performance—there is more to this statement. Because a large fraction of assets are managed professionally, it is clearly impossible for the average *professional* manager to produce a positive alpha, given that no sufficiently large group of counterparties exists that willingly accepts a negative alpha. Although sources questioned the ability of any given manager to consistently produce alpha, they also raised the question of whether the alpha eventually generated, even if positive, was still positive net of management fees.

Second, and more importantly, even if a given asset manager can produce a positive alpha, the magnitude of the alpha is much smaller than the magnitude of returns that can be ascribed to market swings. Consider, for example, the swings in value from market highs at the beginning of 2007 to year-end 2009. During this brief span, the S&P 500 Index lost more than half of its value by March 2009 and finished 2009 at around only 65 percent from the March low. No alpha can compensate for these movements. The period of 2007–2009 was more volatile than usual, but in just over 20 years, there have been at least five periods (1987, 1994,

1997–1998, 2000–2002, 2007–2009) during which market valuations experienced large swings. Market swings are much larger than the (eventually) few percentage points above a benchmark that an investor can hope to gain from active management.

Institutional investors have taken heed. The head of institutional business at a large U.K. management firm noted that some funds are shifting their focus to moving in and out of asset classes in response to the markets. According to this source, "Asset allocation will clearly be a significant driver of returns in the future. Investors have come to realize that changing the manager of, say, European equities from manager A to manager B—which might be painful and costly—is not so important. But the big calls are what matter—for example, a move from emerging markets to commodities or from bonds to real estate. Asset allocation is what makes the difference."

Another source in the United Kingdom concurred, adding that strong growth in the demand for asset allocation advice and products will constitute one of the major changes following the recent market crash because it has become apparent that the performance of various asset classes drives returns. According to this source, "In the last two years, it has become academic if one owns this large-cap stock as opposed to that one, but it is important if one owned large cap as opposed to emerging markets equities. More of a top-down approach is now called for." It boils down to a question of the relative importance of alpha and beta in investment strategies.

Nevertheless, sources agreed that asset allocation was very hard to get right. The CIO at a buffer fund in Sweden said, "One of the lessons we have learned with the events of 2007–2009 is that everyone now knows that asset allocation is more important than security-level portfolio management. But if you get asset allocation wrong, you get it very wrong: It is very difficult to make big bets. There are so many factors to factor in and if you get just one wrong . . . . With hindsight, we knew that we should have sold all equities in mid-2007, versus stock picking; if you analyze firms, it is relatively easy to get it right."

An asset manager in Austria who agreed that asset allocation was indeed a difficult task said,

> The danger is always there that you do not get the asset allocation right. Volatility is high; it is very hard to achieve ideal points in time. If you are too early or too late, performance gets hurt. But our asset allocation funds are done top-down—they are mathematically driven. We do long- and short-term allocations; we measure different risks and how they are correlated. One can do asset allocation and make strong bets, but we make smaller bets. For example, a big bet is 100 percent equities or 0 percent equities. Some are doing this. But what we have seen is that, on average, results from this approach are not better than from the benchmark-driven approach, which makes smaller bets around market weights.

To say that the investment policy explains a large percentage of the variation of returns over time is not to say that manager diversification and implementation fail to add value. A consultant in Europe remarked, "Asset allocation determines the risk and future returns. It is responsible for 80–90 percent of the risk budget; asset managers are responsible for the remaining 10–20 percent. One needs this additional 10–20 percent, especially considering that it is not correlated to the strategic allocation risk."

A consultant in the United States whose clients' assets exceed US$1 trillion added,

> In market situations such as those we have just been through, there is the need to demonstrate added value, to show performance relative to custom benchmarks, and to show value added in manager selection and access. We do an annual analysis that compares the top and bottom quartile clients in terms of performance and identifies what percentage of the performance differential is explained by differences in asset allocation and what percentage is explained by the selection of managers. Although it is absolutely important to get the asset allocation right as most institutional investors embrace broad diversification, our studies show that implementation has become more critical. In our most recent analysis, we found that more than 69 percent of the differential is due to implementation. In certain asset classes, such as private equity and real estate, there can be a more than 1,000 bp differential between the median and 25th percentile managers alone.

Dynamic Asset Allocation

The current discussion on dynamic versus static asset allocation was opened by the late Peter Bernstein in his 2003 paper "Are Policy Portfolios Obsolete?" A policy portfolio is a portfolio that represents the long-term views of an investor; it corresponds to a static global asset allocation. Bernstein argued that asset allocation should follow market changes and become opportunistic, thereby rendering obsolete the notion of a policy portfolio. Bernstein's paper has been widely debated, but judging from the number of times we heard the word "opportunistic" pronounced by sources in describing their asset allocation strategies, it seems to have won some converts. One investment consultant remarked, "What has changed is that with today's volatile markets, switching in and out of asset classes, such as equities and bonds, has become much more compelling."

Among the institutional investors we talked to, twice as many said they had adopted dynamic asset allocation compared with those who said they had not. An investment consultant in northern Europe remarked that, in response to the recent market crash, large institutional investors are becoming more dynamic in their asset allocation. According to this source,

> In the past, investors were observing risk but not steering their asset allocation in response to risk. Investors see themselves as victims in the crisis as opposed to having been active. One area where investors can change is in revisiting asset

allocation. Small funds have the feeling that something is missing, whereas large funds have a notion of what is missing. The latter are going toward a more dynamic, less segmented, and less layered approach in which a consultant sets a benchmark for about three years with, say, 40 percent equities, and so on, plus inflation hedging and interest rate hedging. Then investors look for an internal or external manager to run the portfolio, with no exchange of information between the strategy and the management of the funds, no feedback loop. This process leads to, for example, building a portfolio in commodities when prices are already high or in equities when prices have already rebounded.

The CIO at a pension fund in the financial services industry commented, "For years, we did only strategic asset allocation with occasional rebalancing. We would have gladly stuck to this model if the environment had not changed, but when the game has changed, you need to change your approach. We now rebalance yearly."

CIOs at some institutional investors are moving cautiously toward a more dynamic approach. The CIO at a Dutch fund said,

> As professionals, we are about to recommend to the board of trustees the adoption of a more dynamic approach to asset allocation, not necessarily changing the asset allocation more frequently but doing so more willingly. The classic model was that we must have a static, strategic asset allocation that produces an equilibrium rate of return in the long run. But given the macro environment and the nervousness, we expect very volatile markets going forward. We will advise the trustees to drop static strategic asset allocation, which gives confidence, in favor of . . . reacting more when markets overshoot. The question is how to determine when a market is overshooting. We will use our macro views plus a very basic moving average approach to determine momentum changes. We will follow market behavior.

The CIO at a €23 billion Scandinavian fund said,

> There is now much agreement in the academic literature that where it is possible to add value is in the medium term, the one- to three-year time horizon. Small funds can be run as a dynamic hedge fund, but big funds are by nature long-term investors. We cannot change our asset mix too frequently. It is difficult to get rid of the old model. It is possible to become a bit more dynamic, but we cannot be long in equities one day and short the next. Nevertheless, we will be trying to manage equities more dynamically and also allocating between asset classes, such as fixed income and equity. But we cannot be truly tactical because no big shifts are possible over a three-month period.

Sources remarked that recent large market swings have, in any case, made it difficult to stick to a static asset allocation, even without making a deliberate choice to adopt dynamic asset allocation. A source in the United States commented,

> If you decide to be 50 percent in equities and the market takes you down to 45 percent, do you rebalance? And, if yes, how frequently and by how much? In principle, you want to buy low and sell high. But trustees will say, "We are going through periods when markets are crashing, and you want us to invest another

US$50 million in equities?" The question is, do you rebalance to the policy target or change the policy target? Many are saying that if you have the right target and believe in it, you should ride out the markets; if not, it is like closing the barn door after the horse is out. But people are now less tolerant of risk.

Another source suggested that the lines between strategic and tactical asset allocation are being blurred. According to this source,

> Many [pension] plans will respond to the market crash by making a larger overhaul than what we would normally see. It is not so much that plans will be changing their portfolios more frequently but that they are being pushed into rebalancing more frequently as they try to lower their risk profile. There is now much interest in dynamic "de-risking," but it is not a radical idea. As assets go up and down in relation to liabilities, there is the need to do dynamic de-risking. We have just seen two bear markets within a decade. Investors are likely to take more risk off the table.

Still other sources mentioned that, in addition to market volatility, accounting standards that now require firms to report their pension plan assets and liabilities marked to market on their balance sheet are behind the move to a more frequent review of asset allocation. A source in Germany said,

> Going through a strategic asset allocation exercise and then optimizing over 10–15 years is no longer possible. Strategic asset allocation is still important, but more and more firms want to see asset allocation on a one- to two-year time frame; plus, they want to protect the fund with overlays. About 20–25 percent of German funds now use dynamic asset allocation (DAA) versus 100 percent long term before the most recent crisis. But I would imagine that if the economy improves, the interest in DAA would recede because the use of DAA makes investing more difficult and involves a cost for the client. Doing optimization over 10 years and then responding to annual realizations leads to greater risk aversion because you see more volatility in the short period.

A recent study by *IPE Magazine* ("Off the Record" 2009) found that a large proportion of respondents—46.5 percent—now review their asset allocation yearly; 26.5 percent reported that they undertook a review every three years. Although about 62 percent do not intend to review their asset allocation more frequently because of the financial crisis, 13.5 percent reported that they have decided within the last 12–18 months to review their asset allocation more frequently, and another 13.5 percent said they plan to review it more frequently in the future. The survey reflected the situation at 46 European pension funds with, on average, €10 billion in invested assets.

Alternatives to dynamic asset allocation exist for investors seeking protection against volatility in asset classes. A source at a corporate pension fund in the financial services sector said, "We do not dynamically adapt but have built in an emergency exit from investments if needed. It is an implementation strategy, a sort of dynamic portfolio protection insurance that allows us to switch into cash if the situation calls for it."

Timing Asset Allocation Calls

An important issue in dynamic asset allocation is the timing. Brinson, Singer, and Beebower's 1991 paper on the determinants of portfolio performance has been interpreted by some to mean that about 90 percent of the (variation of) returns of a pension fund is explained by investment policy, but some have observed that this conclusion is not implied by Brinson et al.[4] In particular, it has been observed that, although asset allocation is indeed responsible for a large fraction of returns, investment performance can be explained, and therefore obtained, through the *timing* of asset allocation decisions.

Sources agreed that the timing of an asset allocation decision is critical. An investment consultant in the United States remarked, "It is absolutely important to get asset allocation right, but most effective in generating returns is the timing of the decision." Timing involves having information about when return trends will reverse as well as when the variances and covariances of the various asset classes will change. The classical techniques of time-series analysis cannot shed light on when an asset class will change behavior, invert trends, or change correlation characteristics; these tasks call for financial forecasts based on macroeconomic considerations.

The head of institutional business at a large U.K. manager commented, "Asset allocation calls are the hardest calls to make. The fact is that with fast switching, most get the market timing horribly wrong." This source advocated a greater role for macroeconomics: "In the past, we believed in a Goldilocks economy. In 2008, we had a wake-up call. Diversification models did not work. We are now being forced to go back to the drawing board and see how to make macro views a more significant part of portfolio construction."

Getting the timing wrong in asset allocation is much more serious than getting it wrong in stock selection because no diversification effect exists to mitigate the consequences of the error. In stock picking, a mistake made in selecting or deselecting a particular stock is not critical because of the many stocks (typically) involved; in timing asset classes, the choice is limited to a small number of classes so the consequences of any mistake can be significant.

Indeed, a source at a large corporate pension plan in the United States cited the difficulty with implementing dynamic asset allocation as the motivation for not adopting it. According to this source, "It is extremely difficult to get asset allocation right, especially in the implementation. It is about as difficult as it is for an elephant to dance."

Assuming that one can make correct forecasts, an outstanding question is just how dynamic asset allocation should be. Among our sources, some mentioned rebalancing quarterly, others yearly, others less frequently still. Most consultants we

---

[4]For example, see Nuttall and Nuttall (1998), Ibbotson and Kaplan (2000), and Nuttall (2000).

talked to suggested revisiting asset allocation every one to three years. "Not tactical," one said, "and not 10, 15, or 20 years either. A 20-year horizon is valid for only the overall risk model, the long-term strategic goal."

Another consultant concurred: "Midterm views on asset allocation are becoming more important. The price you pay to get into a security is critical for future returns. We advise clients to review asset allocation every one to three years, but in between, do not close your eyes. Take a medium-term view on how assets are priced, to identify opportunities of valuation in the various asset classes. In the shorter term, tactical allocation can be done by the fund manager, swaying the allocation in relation to the market."

The CIO at a Dutch fund that will recommend abandoning strategic asset allocation said, "It will not be a question of reacting daily or weekly but over a 10-month period. There will be a cost for such an approach. We will be too slow when the market rebalances, so rebounds will be weaker. But the trade-off is less volatility, less vulnerability, and more protection on the downside."

Still, the CIO at a large U.S. corporate fund mentioned that it was not the time frame but the valuation frame that mattered. According to this source,

> In the past, it was held to be wisdom to have a buy-and-hold strategy in equities. But who has a 100-year time horizon with no risk limit? A buy-and-hold strategy did not work in the United States or Japan during the past 10 or 20 years. Timing is fruitless in the short term, the next 3 or 30 minutes. But if you look at the P/E and ask yourself what you expect it to be in the next, say, 5 years. . . . The real meaning of market timing is valuation based; the P/E cannot go up forever. Calculating when the P/E is right requires lots of things, such as the P/E itself, macroeconomic considerations. . . . I believe in market timing, but asking how often you have to reevaluate your asset allocation decisions is asking the wrong question. It is not a question of the time frame but the valuation frame, a price horizon. If there is a big change in price, you look at it immediately.

Dynamic asset allocation has academic backing. Lionel Martellini, scientific director of the EDHEC-Risk Institute, commented, "Academic research has shown that optimal strategic long-term allocation benchmarks are time varying in the presence of stochastic opportunity sets. In particular, unexpected changes in risk premiums and interest rate levels—as well as changes in volatility levels in incomplete market settings—rationally trigger changes in the asset mix."

Not everyone is a fan of dynamic asset allocation. An asset manager in the United States commented, "Asset switching subtracts from returns. It costs a ton of dollars and aggravates the problem. Look at what happened in late 2008 when all valuations went down together. An alternative is to run multiple portfolios in a single portfolio."

Global Tactical Asset Allocation

Global tactical asset allocation (GTAA) exploits predictable short- to medium-term changes in the expected returns of different asset classes. If the forecast of returns of an asset class increases (decreases) with respect to other classes, that asset class is tactically overweighted (underweighted) with respect to the long-term weights.

The head of a multiemployer pension fund in Austria said, "We have now had several securities market crises within the space of a decade. The structure of portfolios will not work as in the past. We need to be more active with decisions and, in certain cases, make decisions on a daily basis. But we need to keep in mind the volatility. Daily levels of volatility are now at levels that used to be typical of volatility at one month. We will use more tactical asset allocation for hedging purposes, hedging all kinds of risk—beta risk, currency risk. . . ."

The CIO at a Dutch pension fund said, "We don't have a fixed horizon, such as quarterly, for performing tactical asset allocation but do it only if there is a basis or a reason."

Still, many sources are skeptical regarding global tactical asset allocation. For some, it is a question of size, which makes this strategy difficult to use. Others suggested that GTAA should be used only in special circumstances, such as when market valuations are extreme. Others noted that the high volume of transactions involved in implementing GTAA compromises the expected payoff.

The CIO at a private-sector fund in Europe said, "As attention shifts to preserving capital in an unstable environment, you need to make macroeconomic forecasts rather than focus on beating the benchmark. This approach introduces the question of timing, but there is so much we do not know yet. The question is, How frequently do we want to do tactical asset allocation? We are not relative value traders. We do not believe in daily trading. It is our perception that GTAA mandates with a large volume of transactions have had disappointing results. Our view is that you can do GTAA sometimes, when markets are extremely valued."

The CIO of a Swedish buffer fund remarked, "Some external managers have been doing GTAA, trading daily, but it is not easy to make money with this strategy. It worked well during the crisis, but it was quite disastrous in 2009."

In February of 2009, the Swedish buffer fund AP1 (First Swedish National Pension Fund) announced that it would be abandoning global tactical asset allocation to concentrate on what it considered its core activity, strategic asset allocation. In introducing the change, the fund's managing director said that it would reduce the number of transactions, thereby creating the conditions for a higher total return in the long term.[5]

---

[5]See Investment & Pensions Europe (2009a).

The insight behind both GTAA and GDAA is that markets have become efficient at the level of individual stocks (at least in developed markets) but are still inefficient at the level of asset classes. In other words, the returns of and covariances between asset classes and indices are more predictable than the returns of individual assets. For example, Amenc, Malaise, Martellini, and Sfeir (2003) wrote, "There is now a consensus in empirical finance that asset class returns are, to some extent, predictable. On the other hand, 30 years of academic studies have shown that there is little evidence of predictability in the specific components of stock returns in the absence of private information."

A number of points should be noted. First, it is obvious that the return and covariance characteristics of individual assets are much noisier than the corresponding return and covariance characteristics of asset classes that are broad aggregates of individual assets. For example, studies using methods based on random matrix theory have shown that covariance matrices are very noisy.[6] See, for example, Plerou, Gopikrishnan, Rosenow, Nunes Amaral, Guhr, and Stanley (2002).

The point here is that, even after filtering noise, asset classes and indices are more predictable than individual assets for many reasons. One explanation is cointegration. It is well known that portfolios are more predictable than individual assets because of cointegration effects. For example, Lo and MacKinlay (1990) observed that predictability is present in size-sorted portfolios in the sense that the returns of portfolios of large-cap stocks are predictors of portfolios of small-cap stocks. The predictability exhibited by size-sorted portfolios is short-term predictability, possibly as a result of short-term delays in the diffusion of news.

It is difficult, however, to find the common underlying intuition as to why returns on different asset classes—including assets as varied as stocks, bonds, and hedge funds—are predictable. Each asset class might exhibit different sources of predictability, and it might be futile to search for a generalized intuition on the predictability of asset classes.

Whether the widespread diffusion of GTAA and GDAA will make markets more efficient in the classical sense or shift the notion of volatility on to a different time scale remains to be seen. Stated differently, the main risk is the risk of the inversion of local trends. This consideration is implicit in the comments on the difficulty of timing in tactical asset allocation. GTAA is based on forecasting local trends with time horizons in the range of a few months. Although these trends are by nature opportunistic and subject to reversal, forecasting trend reversals is difficult.

---

[6]Random matrix theory is widely used in probability theory and statistics. In finance, random matrix theory is used to determine the number of factors in a linear factor model.

Expanding the Investable Universe

As mentioned earlier, a third development in investment management, related to both global tactical asset allocation and global dynamic asset allocation, consists of an expanded investable universe. More than 10 years ago, at year-end 1998, Towers Watson (2009) estimated that 90 percent of all pension assets in the seven largest national pension markets were allocated to just two asset classes—stocks and bonds. The split was 60 percent in stocks and 30 percent in bonds.

In a widely cited paper, Sharpe (1992) argued that the returns on styles (i.e., subsets of a universe of stocks based on stock characteristics) are responsible for 97 percent of a portfolio's return variation. Fama and French (1992) carried Sharpe's analysis a step further and suggested that just three factors (or styles) were needed to explain almost all stock return variation. The factors are the market, size, and book to market. Carhart (1997) added a fourth factor—momentum.

Therefore, asset classes evolved to include not only assets that are intrinsically different but also assets that represent trading strategies. In this sense, styles or asset classes are defined by low correlation with other asset classes and possibly by forecastability of returns. The need for uncorrelated asset classes plays an important role in classical static asset allocation based on diversification. In the context of dynamic asset allocation, however, investors should no longer rely on uncorrelated asset classes but, instead, on the ability to exploit dynamic effects ultimately related to investors' ability to make forecasts, albeit relative forecasts. This approach is the essence of dynamic hedging.

Among the different asset classes that have been added, hedge funds are particularly important. Hedge funds use classical asset classes, such as stocks, bonds, currencies, or cash, to create trading strategies based on properties of the market that are, in principle, uncorrelated with the market's ups and downs.

The definition of an asset class is not always clear-cut. In the Editor's Corner of the *Financial Analysts Journal*, Richard Ennis (2009) observed that the notion of asset classes is blurred. Ennis advocates a parsimonious set of asset classes, in contrast to what he sees as an unnecessary proliferation of poorly defined asset classes. The problem with defining asset classes is not a problem of ontology but is ultimately related to the methodologies used in making forecasts and in forming asset allocation strategies.

We asked sources how they will be allocating their assets following the recent market crash. Not surprisingly, many said that investors will be taking risk off the table as well as reducing exposure to equities and, in particular, domestic equities for sources in the United Kingdom and the United States. (As equity markets started to recover by mid-2009, investors were reevaluating the attractiveness of equities as an asset class.) Sources also said that investors will be reducing their investments in complex products with hidden fees, such as funds of funds. In contrast, our sources also reported that investors will (1) increase diversification and (2) be more opportunistic—for example, investing in distressed debt and real estate based on the low valuations in those asset classes.

Regarding greater diversification, the asset classes to which sources said investors will be turning are (listed in descending order of the number of mentions) emerging markets equities, bonds, private equity (often through direct investments), infrastructure (typical of continental Europe), hedge funds, and, more generally, nonpublic assets, including intellectual property rights. The head of a London-based manager said, "We will see the continued growth of and diversity in the alternatives business—for example, commodities, real estate, distressed credit, and infrastructure—being done with asset allocation."

Sources at a large public-sector institutional investor in North America mentioned that they will be shifting investments into nonpublic markets because of recent historical volatility. One source at this investor, which manages 80 percent of its assets internally, said, "We are shifting from public to nonpublic asset classes for returns, cash flows, and stability of returns. We have set a long-term target of less than 50 percent public asset classes and more than 50 percent private and will not be changing this shortly. We are long-term investors."

The CIO of a large second-pillar fund in northern Europe remarked, "What we have been doing is to give more focus to real returns but out of unusual assets, such as infrastructure, private equity, and other alternatives, such as intellectual property, that we manage ourselves."[7] The source added that these investments are quite limited.

The question about whether nonpublic or unusual assets should generate higher or more stable returns than public assets was hotly debated by our sources. The head of a large international asset management firm said, "It is an acceptable assumption but with God knows how many caveats. Where investors have long-term liabilities that can be matched with long-term assets, why pay the liquidity premium for assets you do not need in the short term? The potential for performance should be greater in illiquid markets because greater inefficiencies exist there. The problem is to make sure the investor is not getting only leveraged beta."

The CIO of a large corporate fund in the United Kingdom said,

> Those coming into nonpublic assets now are coming in a bit late. We have been in private equity for 10 years, with an in-house private equity team. What we have noticed is that the premium on illiquid assets has been down for a few years. It has become clear that nonpublic asset classes are getting more from leverage than from the investment itself. In addition, illiquid assets are more difficult to value. It might appear to be a real win–win investment; valuation appears to be smooth, and if you do modeling, it looks good. But if you find yourself in the situation of having to sell, valuation is stretched.

[7]In the parlance of life-cycle finance, funds may be categorized in terms of which "pillars" of retirement security they represent, with U.S. Social Security being typical of the "first pillar."

The source added an additional consideration, "Reality might bear out the hypothesis in the long-term game, but what if the plan sponsor goes out of business or something else happens? This is especially important in today's environment. Given the need to mark to market pension assets and liabilities and put them on the balance sheet, people in the [private-sector] pension fund industry are playing a different game now from the point of view of risk tolerance. Time horizons are tighter."

Other sources questioned whether nonpublic assets would deliver better risk-adjusted returns than public assets because of the embedded risk. The CIO of a large public-sector fund in the United States said, "Clearly, there is the need to diversify. We now understand that domestic and nondomestic equities are one asset class, not two. In 2008, we saw that the whole world was correlated. We have to achieve diversification, but we have no history on nonpublic assets. Even the best have had difficulty in private equity."

Some suggested that, following the crisis, it is time to return to basics. A source at a Swiss asset management firm remarked, "There are paradigm shifts from time to time, such as the repackaging of subprime mortgages into AAA vehicles. But following market turmoil, the bulk of the portfolio needs to be back to the basics." According to this source, the firm's ability to limit investor losses in the recent market crash was the result of several factors: It did not chase what was in fashion, such as reverse/convertible notes or structured products; it had no blowups on the counterparty side; and it was able to make decent investment decisions, such as choosing products that could be used for limiting downside risk.

Perhaps we will have to wait until the next crisis to understand which strategy delivered!

Asset Allocation and the Individual Investor

If institutional investors have, to a large extent, concluded that asset allocation decisions, as opposed to outperformance relative to a given benchmark, account for the largest part of returns and will thus be reviewing their asset allocation decisions more dynamically, where does that leave the individual investor? One source remarked, "Institutional investors know that they get the most value (80–90 percent) through asset allocation rather than through the asset manager. It is the retail investor who believes that he or she gets value through the asset manager." But sources said that "shell-shocked" retail investors are losing their appetite for mutual funds and, in particular, for equities.

Awareness of the problem has led pension funds with defined-contribution plans and asset managers to design retail investment products that offer some protection against wide market swings. To do so, they are designing products that automatically switch in and out of asset classes as valuations change.

A source in Europe that is marketing asset allocation funds to retail investors remarked, "Asset allocation products are becoming more important for the retail investor for whom pure, single-asset class, long-only bond or equity funds have lost their attractiveness. They might remain as bricks in a fund of funds, but one-asset-class portfolios are now sold with an overlay for downside protection."

Target-date, life-cycle, and lifestyle funds belong to the family of retail products that use asset allocation strategies. Life-cycle investment funds are based on the idea that investors can assume investment risk when they are young because they have time to recover losses but that they need to reduce investment risk when approaching retirement because they no longer have the time to recover losses. The dilemma of those entering retirement in March 2009 is an example of how a lifetime investment can be compromised by the retirement date. A rule of thumb approximately implemented in many life-cycle funds is that the percentage of stocks invested in should be equal to 100 minus the age of the person. Yale University's Robert Shiller (2006), however, has called this rule suboptimal.

Although life-cycle funds are being increasingly adopted by sponsors of defined-contribution plans in the United States and elsewhere, some sources suggested that forecasted valuations should also be taken into consideration in determining the asset allocation of these products. The head of a multiemployer fund in central Europe remarked, "Changing the asset allocation in a portfolio solely on the basis of the member's age is complete nonsense, as are other strictly mechanical portfolio management concepts. Automatically decreasing equity investments in a portfolio along with the age of a member of a pension plan fully exposes the member to market risk. Why," this source asked, "should a pensioner suffer because he retires in a market with low bond yields? There is no correlation between the age of a pension plan member and how the market behaves."

A source at a U.K. asset management firm remarked that new lifestyle products allow a certain level of adaptation to both investment objective and markets. According to this source, "A key trend in retail is the development of lifestyle products with dynamic asset allocation that adapts to changes in objectives versus, in the past, target-date funds that switch as the participant ages (for example, Age A = Fund X, Age B = Fund Y). Lifestyle products are now supported by a professional asset allocator or staff that takes into account the objectives of the investor, a macro perspective, and a certain level of adaptation to markets. But because timing can go so horribly wrong, it is not such a good idea to allow the retail investor to get in and out of markets quickly."

Throwing Out the Old Staples of Asset Management?

An industry observer commented on investment management today: "Old certainties, old ways of doing business in investment management are breaking down, changing. The fourth quarter of 2008 and the first quarter of 2009 were traumatizing. We have been through a period the likes of which we had not seen before. The industry is now in a period of reflection and contemplation. Everything is open for reassessment."

As discussed earlier, the growing recognition of the predominant role of asset allocation in investment management has produced a change in the classical investment management model based on Markowitz's modern portfolio theory (MPT). One of the consequences of modern portfolio theory is the fund separation theorem, which maintains that every investor will hold the same portfolio of risky securities. In modern portfolio theory, the portfolio held by all investors is the market portfolio formed by all investable securities held in proportion to their market capitalization.

This conclusion has been criticized from various points of view. Ross (1976) proposed multifactor models and showed that, under appropriate conditions, a fund separation theorem holds in the sense that investors choose among a small number of funds. This theorem forms the basis of passive investment strategies.

The choice of funds in which to invest, and the consequent asset allocation, is central to this investment strategy. The core–satellite approach, which ultimately depends on fund separation, consists of a core that is managed passively plus a number of actively managed satellites for alpha generation. The rationale of the core–satellite approach is that it gives the best of both worlds. The core is passive and delivers beta returns at a low cost; active management fees are paid only for that fraction of assets with which it is believed that value can be added in the form of outperformance relative to a benchmark. The modern evolution of the core–satellite model is to apply the principles of dynamic asset allocation to the core, which need not be a passive market portfolio but can be formed more efficiently by a number of appropriately chosen indices (see Amenc, Malaise, and Martellini 2004).

We asked sources how they evaluated the core–satellite approach in light of recent market events. Most consultants agreed that a shift away from the core–satellite approach has occurred, although the core–satellite approach might remain for equity and bond portfolios. Some of the reasons cited are a loss of risk appetite among investors that is working against active management (the satellite part of a core–satellite approach), growing diversification among asset classes, and the rise of unconstrained, absolute-return mandates.

A source at a U.S. firm advising on almost US$600 billion in investable assets remarked, "A prudent shift away from a core–satellite model is under way. The math never really made great sense. Investors need a strong feeling about managers to outsource risk to a manager. They are now taking a more balanced approach to rebalancing to lower risk in active products. There is a benefit to diversifying among sources of alpha as well as of beta, and the core–satellite approach does not take advantage of this diversification. That is why a move is occurring toward selecting managers whose risks/returns are uncorrelated."

Among institutional investors, more than half said that either a core–satellite approach was never part of their investment approach or they are moving away from it. This result was particularly pronounced among the large northern European funds that typically do not use consultants in asset allocation. Reasons cited by institutional investors for moving away from a core–satellite approach included a shift in accent toward capital preservation, greater diversification with alternatives, and the use of unconstrained, absolute-return mandates.

The CIO of an industrywide fund in Holland said, "Using a core–satellite approach would mean creating active portfolios on purpose. Our conclusion is that active equity has disappointed since 2007. Today, we look at asset allocation to equities and decide where we want to be and, in response to this, the active–passive choice follows. For example, if we want to be in U.S. or European large cap, there is a lot of research available, so active managers cannot add too much. But in Japanese small cap, an active manager can add value."

The CIO at a U.K. pension fund said, "We are using core–satellite in equities and bonds, which represents 85 percent of our invested assets. Our objective is to diversify away from equity and bond beta and adopt an absolute-return–like target with alternatives, such as private equity, infrastructure, and funds of hedge funds."

While acknowledging that the core–satellite approach had made a contribution to asset allocation, one source noted the need for a more integrated approach than that provided by the core–satellite approach. According to this source, "The core–satellite approach was useful in that it relied on specialization and expertise in asset classes, such as emerging markets. But it was a mistake in the sense that, after specialization, you do not do anything else. The mistake was not developing the capacity to understand the trade-off between asset classes."

Nevertheless, some sources that use a core–satellite approach will continue to do so. The CIO of a corporate fund in Holland said, "We do not think that managers can consistently beat the benchmark in developed markets. Through style diversification, however, we believe that we attain a result that gives us the benchmark yield plus a compensation for the management fee that would be better than the result from a passive manager."

A core–satellite approach involves choosing or designing a benchmark that will serve as the basis for manager selection and performance measurement. We asked sources if rumors of the demise of benchmarking are accurate. "Benchmarking is not dead," the CIO at a large U.K. manager said, "but it is rightly now being given less importance. You do not pay pensions out of relative performance. The question for pension funds is, Has my funding ratio gone up or down?"

A source at a large northern European fund that manages assets in-house concurred: "The real benchmark is not what the equity markets are doing but asset growth versus liabilities. Suppose the market is down 20 percent and the manager is down only 18 percent—but you cannot pay pensions with −18 percent. The whole concept of running money is very different from the notion of a benchmark."

The CIO at a corporate pension fund in central Europe remarked,

Benchmark thinking is no longer of interest. It was of interest when you were looking at the long term, but with today's level of volatility, we are looking at short-term developments. This environment calls for short-term reactions but based on a macro view with limits. For example, when a predetermined limit is reached, we must be ready to act quickly. We need to manage risk on the downside as well as optimize the downside risk and the upside in every market, so we adapt portfolios to react on what is happening in the market. For example, in our bond portfolios, we need to have a view on the relative value of government and corporate bonds to understand what is under- or overvalued at any particular moment. The time horizon depends on what is happening in any specific asset class. Take currency; we look at it more frequently but also have a strategic view. We watch the limit set by our strategic view and are ready to act.

Another CIO in Europe said,

We come from a fairly stable environment. We have been through a long cycle in which the average profit on holding an equity portfolio generated acceptable revenues. What is now new is that volatility and instability are up and the idea of sticking to a benchmark as it moves up and down and generates 2 percent returns is not enough anymore. We now discuss with asset managers how to outperform the markets when markets go up and ways to preserve capital when markets go down. Our attention has shifted to preserving capital. Rather than beat the benchmark, we need to forecast market turns. It is a question of market timing.

The industry itself is questioning the wisdom of having played by benchmark rules. The CIO at a U.K. manager said, "The fund management industry did harm to itself—and the government helped—in putting all the effort into controlling risk relative to a benchmark. More modern funds are more dynamic versus the use of benchmarks and periodic rebalancing."

As mentioned earlier, active and passive management play a central role in the core–satellite approach. Although positions on the relative merits of active and passive management continue to resemble, in some aspects, a battle of faiths, it is fair to say that a consensus has been reached: Active management does not add value in developed efficient markets (at least in some parts, such as large cap), but active management does add value in inefficient or emerging markets. Sources also mentioned that a time element is involved and that active management delivers better outperformance in some market situations. The head of institutional business at a U.K. manager remarked, "Passive management will have a very strong role in the future. Passive will go up, double from 20–30 percent today to 50 percent for core regions. If you take the U.S. or Japanese large cap and look back at the last decade, no one has been able to consistently outperform. This fact is the key behind the BlackRock/BGI [Barclays Global Investors] merger. The active space will be reduced. Active managers will be pushed into managing with higher tracking errors, and in a parallel trend, active managers will be competing directly with absolute-return managers, such as hedge funds."

But the need for active managers to set the price was emphasized by a source at a large indexer. According to this source, "Passive management is a free-ride strategy; it piggybacks on active management. You need to have active managers out there, and they need to be paid. It is a question of balance. Twenty years ago, the split was 90/10 active/passive; 10 years ago it was 70/30, and it stayed there until recently when passive started going up again. Do we need active managers to set price levels? Definitely, but a lot fewer than in the past. Thirty percent would be adequate to set a price level; it is a question of balance."

The CIO at an asset management firm cast the argument in the framework of alpha and beta, "There are two different points of view on active versus passive. Active has disappointed; investors have been incredibly dissatisfied over a number of years. But with passive management, indices, or exchange-traded funds (ETFs), returns have been pretty horrible. The question is, How much do you want to buy into the passive beta?"

Although some sources mentioned that they will be moving toward a full separation of alpha and beta, other sources said that too much emphasis has been put on alpha. The CIO at one of the world's largest pension funds remarked, "We are moving away from the concept of alpha. Alpha is a difficult asset management concept. As a pension fund, we are interested in absolute returns in real terms, not alpha. We have two portfolios: one to produce stable returns and one, growth. Our view is that you do not have to outperform a benchmark every quarter. We take a long-term view of fulfilling the goals for our clients, the plan members."

In Chapter 7, institutional investors identify their biggest challenge as the need to deliver the pension promise. Clearly, it is understandable that institutional investors would like to have absolute returns to match their liabilities. But some sources were skeptical about the ability of the investment management industry to deliver. One investment professional said, "Absolute-return products are a thing of the past; the possibility of guaranteeing returns does not exist."

3. Risk Management Revisited

We asked sources if the crash of 2008 will turn out to be a blip or have a lasting effect. Sources agreed that this market crash, unlike the crashes of 1987, 1994, and 2000, will have a lasting effect. In particular, as one source remarked, "Investors are now materially more intolerant of risk. They have been burnt and will reduce their exposure to market risk." The source cited the Conference Board's 2009 (Tonello and Rabimov 2009) report on asset allocation and portfolio composition that showed a more than 20 percent decline in managed assets at U.S. pension funds, life insurance, foundations, and mutual funds for year-end 2008 compared with year-end 2007.[8] The source added, "As a result of the crash of 1929, both economic and investment behavior were materially different throughout the 1930s. This response was not the case with the crash of 1987—which was a blip—nor with the decline of 1994 or even with the crash of 2000. This crash [2008] is different; it is more significant, and the repercussions will be more lasting."

What went amiss with risk management in 2008? The CIO of a U.K. public-sector fund commented,

> In March 2008, views of asset management houses did not include the forthcoming market crash. It was very difficult to stand out from the crowd and call the crash. It is almost better to be average and wrong. I had the feeling that something was wrong. I remember talking to people and saying, "How can people be offered a mortgage that is 120 percent the value of the house?" And I was getting 10 solicitations for credit cards every two weeks! The problem is the way we look at risk; there was the risk that the market was going to fall off a cliff, but it was not being considered properly. In value at risk analysis, it always seems to be the 1 percent that creates the real damage. It was not so much a question of the appetite for risk; people just did not see the risk. The volatility in the indices was so low for so long. But, as Minsky said, if anything has been going steadily up for so long, it is bound to blow up soon.[9]

---

[8]According to the Conference Board's (Tonello and Rabimov 2009) report, managed assets at U.S. pension funds, life insurance, foundations, and mutual funds fell to $22 trillion by year-end 2008 from $28.3 trillion at year-end 2007.

[9]Hyman Minsky analyzed how capitalistic economies are prone to boom-and-bust cycles—periods of apparently strong growth based on easy credit followed by crises. See Minsky 1982; Minsky 1986.

Risk? What Risk?

Sources agreed that it was not only market risk that had not been properly considered prior to the 2008 crash but also liquidity risk, counterparty risk, and systemic risk, as well as leverage. The CIO of a Swedish buffer fund observed, "What people missed was liquidity. The management of liquidity risk was the big failure. Counterparty risk, credit risk was also missed, and to some degree, market risk in the portfolios was missed."

Risk is uncertainty. The task of risk management is not to predict future events with certainty (an impossible task in any case) but to measure just how uncertain predictions are—that is to say, to estimate the likelihood and the magnitude of losses. In investment management, the task of risk management is to dynamically quantify the amount of risk present in strategies and portfolios and to identify strategies to bring the level of risk back to the desired amount.

Market risk is the risk that the value of an investment (or trading) portfolio will decrease due to an adverse change in the value of a market risk factor. There is market risk at different time horizons. At short time horizons, there is the risk of unpredictable large downward price movements. Examples include the crash of 1987 or the market crash following 9/11. Both crashes saw markets recover their losses in a relatively short period of time. But the crash of 1929 was followed by a 20-year period during which prices failed to return to their 1929 highs. There is also the risk of prolonged stagnant markets or markets characterized by slow but continuous downward price movements, without being preceded by a crash. An example is the 16-year period from 1966 to 1982.

The need to consider liquidity risk is, sources agreed, one of the big lessons learned from the recent crisis. Liquidity has more than one meaning in economics. A financial market is said to be liquid if transactions can be executed rapidly at a fair price. An illiquid market is one in which it is difficult to find buyers or sellers, thereby forcing the buyer or seller to execute his or her order at a price not aligned with the fair price of the assets to be traded. Liquidity risk is the risk that the ability to perform transactions at a fair price will become severely reduced. "In the absence of liquidity," one source commented, "pricing becomes academic because there is no market."

Liquidity dried up in the summer of 2007 as highly leveraged investors were forced to sell assets to cover margin calls. One source who identified the failure to manage liquidity risk as *the* big failure of the most recent crisis observed, "With lack of liquidity, all parameters moved; what was considered liquid became illiquid. There was too little time to get out of positions."

Counterparty risk also forced its way to the top of investors' concerns in 2008. As investors adopted hedging and trading strategies based on derivative contracts, investors became increasingly exposed to counterparty risk. In addition, this risk was concentrated in just a few institutions. When Lehman Brothers collapsed in September 2008, investors had an unpleasant wake-up call. As one investment consultant reported, "In the wake of Lehman's collapse, the only thing investors were asking about was risk management at the fund level, the counterparty risk on derivatives, and is my fund blowing up?"

Leverage and Systemic Risk

Among the various causes of the crisis, leverage is singled out as an important trigger. The CIO at a large U.S. public-sector fund said, "The biggest lessons learned from events as of mid-2007 were (1) leverage cuts both ways and (2) risk models did not take this into consideration. Every time we move above 10/1 leverage, there is a danger. So, when people go to 30/1 and 40/1 leverage, it becomes life threatening. Such high levels of leverage were behind Long-Term Capital Management (LTCM), Orange County, Bear Stearns, Lehman Brothers, and other toxic assets." The source added,

> No one knew how much leverage was out there. We have been very vocal about the lack of transparency in transactions. There is leverage on leverage. Banks were not keeping records on this leverage. Consider AIG's [American International Group] swap book. Some of the brightest people looked at it, were told that the book balanced, but did not question this information. Some private equity firms were considering purchasing the business but were not able to figure out the value of the derivatives on the books. Valuation estimates went from US$30 billion to US$60 billion to US$120 billion or even US$140 billion. The problem was the granularity on the contracts. Those persons who looked at the books and assigned a range of valuations missed by up to fivefold. There is the need for transparency on the underlying security to figure out the leverage of a firm.

An asset manager remarked,

> Investors and asset managers alike do not understand leverage and its effects as much as we think we do. The problem is both a lack of knowledge and a lack of data. I cannot believe anyone understood the layers of leverage in collateralized debt obligations squared (CDOs-squared)[10] and collateralized debt obligations cubed (CDOs-cubed).[11] When you deconstruct the instruments to see how they were built, there was a lot of complicated engineering. It was very hard for even the smartest to tear apart a CDO-cubed to determine the triggers and how they would behave. There was an appetite for extreme leverage.

---

[10]A CDO-squared is a collateralized debt obligation (CDO) in which the collateral consists of tranches of other CDOs. Banks have used one type of CDO, a collateralized loan obligation, in which the collateral is backed by bank loans. Basically, a CDO allows banks and other financial entities to transfer credit risk.

[11]A CDO-cubed is a CDO in which collateral is backed by tranches of CDOs and CDOs-squared.

Systemic risk is the other risk that reared its head in the recent crisis. In finance, systemic risk is the risk of collapse of an entire financial market or entire financial system, as opposed to risk associated with any one individual entity, group, or component of a system. Systemic risk can be defined as global financial system instability, typically caused by interdependencies in a market or a system that can cause a cascade of failures, potentially bankrupting or bringing down the entire market or the entire system. The CIO at a large Scandinavian public-sector fund said,

> Systemic risk was not considered. A key issue is that risk aversion was not factored in. It was considered that diversification would work. People forgot that markets are not exogenous; there is interconnectivity of markets and of economies. The whole economic system was touched. You can point a finger to important political decisions and to huge policy mistakes, such as the U.S. housing market. People were happy to take good returns, huge returns, but forgot that long-term normal returns cannot be double the growth of the economy.

Given the amount of risk and investment managers' inability to make correct forecasts, investors are turning to risk management and, where needed, are making greater use of hedging than before. The CIO at a private-sector pension fund said,

> In asset/liability management or balance sheet management, we do Monte Carlo simulations and use derivatives. In the fourth quarter of 2007, we hedged our portfolios with plain vanilla derivatives, such as equity puts to protect the coverage ratio. Unlike some other pension funds, our coverage remained stable. The counterparty risk was solved by using collateral. We accepted equities and bonds as collateral and came out okay, but those who asked for cash had to pay interest and put cash in money market funds. But the money market funds invested in structured products that went down the drain; it was a loss-making business.

Fat Tails and the Short-Term View

"The need to calculate tail risk is an important lesson learned from recent market turbulence," a source at a Swiss asset management firm said. Tail risk can be understood as the risk that an asset or a portfolio of assets moves more than three standard deviations from its current price. A distribution is said to be fat tailed if the probability of large events is higher than that in a normal bell-shaped (Gaussian) distribution. At short time horizons, the distribution of stock returns is not normal but is fat tailed, although the variance of return distributions remains finite. Established in academic studies (see, for example, Rachev and Mittnik 2000; Rachev, Menn, and Fabozzi 2005), the fat-tailed state of the variance of return distributions at short time horizons should have been known to investment practitioners.

The CIO of a large U.S. public-sector fund remarked, "We use correlations and noticed that, during recent crises, correlations were not static but moved. But we did not think that tails were so dismally fat. In the space of six years, we had the equivalent of Pearl Harbor (i.e., 11 September 2001) and 1929 (i.e., events from mid-2007 to the first quarter of 2009). That makes two black swan events, but we need a better concept than black swans."[12]

An interplay between fat tails and correlations occurs. Because markets are correlated, diversification can be only partially effective at reducing risk. In other words, all assets partially move together. In addition, in the presence of fat tails, a much larger number of assets is required for diversification.

Given that returns are fat tailed, correlation is only an approximation. The concept of linear correlation cannot be used with confidence when variables are fat tailed. The presence of fat tails in the distribution of stock returns implies that linear correlation coefficients do not correctly measure the covariation between stock returns. To correctly measure the covariation, other statistical tools are called for. The most popular one is the copula function.[13]

Because of the fat-tailed distribution of individual assets and the global inter-dependence among assets, broad aggregates (e.g., the S&P 500 Index or the Russell 1000 Index) and even entire asset classes exhibit considerable volatility and correlation with one another along with the distribution of their returns also being fat tailed.

Trend Inversion and the Failure of Diversification

Diversification is said to be the investor's only free lunch. Although Merton (1971) showed that, in a dynamic environment, investors will not only diversify but also dynamically choose what he calls *hedging portfolios*, diversification remains a major tool for portfolio risk management. It is known, however, that the power of diversification is not constant. The head of a multiemployer pension fund in central Europe said, "We want returns above inflation, and so we need a certain risk composition. You need to ask from a macro point of view if your correlation works."

Diversification seems to fail when it is needed most. A popular way of describing the recent crash is to say that "all correlations went to 1.0." In fact, academic studies have shown that, in moments of crisis, the level of correlation increases (see, for example, Longin and Solnik 2001, which refers to correlations among national equity market indices). In the recent crisis, risky asset classes did seem to correlate more highly than usual; the only asset classes with good returns were government bonds (in countries with reasonably stable government balance sheets) and cash.

---

[12]The black swan is a reference to the writing of Nassim Taleb (2007), who used the term to explain the existence of rare events that are difficult to predict but have a major impact on financial decision making. For a critical evaluation of the black swan theory, see Focardi and Fabozzi (2009).

[13]The copula function is used to determine the dependence structure of a multivariate probability distribution. It is based on Sklar's Theorem, which states that any joint probability distribution can be written as a functional link (i.e., a copula function) between its marginal distributions.

It is possible, however, that the perception of spiking correlations is superficial and fails to capture the essence of the crisis. Is the 57 percent drop in the value of the S&P 500 from its peak in 2007 to its trough in March 2009 explained by an increase in correlations between equities and other asset classes? Clearly not. Is the drop explained by a spike in the correlation between the constituent stocks in the index? Possibly, but it is an unsatisfying explanation, and better models are needed to explain this behavior.

Of course, if prices follow random walks and an increase occurs in correlation among asset classes, prices of all asset classes will go up or down together and diversification will be less effective. An increase in correlation either among or within asset classes, however, does not increase the likelihood of a prolonged drop in stock prices. A 57 percent drop in the value of the S&P 500 in a random walk at current levels of volatility is an unlikely event—not impossible but unlikely.

It might be beneficial to look for a different or at least a complementary explanation. This search requires the identification of models that can better explain what occurred. One explanation is fat tails. If returns are fat tailed, then prices are more likely to experience large drops. Another explanation is a reversal of trends or "drifts"—that is, prices are not modeled as random walks but as a sequence of segments of random walks, some of which have positive drifts and others, negative drifts. Because this model shifts among different regimes (i.e., drifts), it is referred to as a regime-switching model. The prototype of regime-switching models was proposed by Hamilton (1989). In Hamilton's model, correlations play a minor role. Instead, the drop is explained as a reversal of drifts. Suppose two different models of the market are built with a breakpoint (or point of inflection) at a given moment in time. In one model, correlation changes at the breakpoint; in the other model, the direction of the drift changes at the breakpoint. Theoretically, we would then choose the model with the highest probability evaluated on the sample.

One response to the bursting of the technology, media, and telecommunications bubble in 2000 was to broaden the universe of investable assets. But, as the crash of 2008 showed, this strategy proved ineffective. In "When Diversification Failed," Ben Inker (2008), CIO at the U.S. asset management firm GMO (Grantham, Mayo, Van Otterloo & Co.), gave an explanation of the failure of diversification in a GMO newsletter. Inker wrote, "In 2007, the world saw the most profound bubble in risk assets ever seen, [and as a consequence], there was no way that portfolio construction techniques could have reduced the size of the overall losses."

Inker argued that diversification failed in 2007 because an inversion of the risk–return trade-off occurred, a phenomenon that diversification cannot mitigate. Inker suggested that a key risk factor that investors should look at is *price risk*, which is whether stocks are over- or underpriced. When the market is, on average, overvalued by a large measure, a strong risk of price declines exists. Among sources, there was broad agreement that the timing of asset allocation decisions is important in explaining returns (see Chapter 2); however, sources agreed that forecasting the timing of inversion is very difficult.

Measuring Risk

Value at risk (VaR) is a widely used method for measuring market risk. Much of the criticism of risk management's failure to deal with the recent crisis is centered on the shortcomings of VaR.[14] Perhaps the best known shortcoming is the fact that VaR is not subadditive. This fact means that the global VaR of the union of two portfolios, or two trading desks, can be larger than the sum of the VaRs of each portfolio or trading desk.[15] This shortcoming is related to the fact that VaR is a confidence interval that gives the maximum possible loss with a given probability. Intuitively, that means VaR is the percentage of times that losses exceed a given threshold. This measure, however, does not specify the size of the loss in excess of a given threshold, only the frequency of such losses.

For example, consider two portfolios, A and B, whose daily losses recorded over a long time series of 1,000 days exceed US$1 million 5 percent of the time—that is, 50 days. Suppose that when losses of portfolio A exceed US$1 million, they remain in the range of US$1.2 million to US$1.5 million, whereas losses of portfolio B, when they exceed US$1 million, may be up to US$5 million as a result of the presence of fat tails. Intuitively, the two portfolios do not have the same risk, but they have the same VaR. This issue is clearly a major shortcoming of VaR because some returns will be fat tailed.

The CIO at a multiemployer fund in Europe said, "We use classical VaR and always keep in mind that all figures from models are information for decision making, not a prediction for the future. We take a strategic view; the future cannot be predicted. But model results allow us to look at the past and reason on the future."

---

[14]VaR is a single-number measure of risk based on confidence intervals that specify events associated with a certain probability. VaR is the maximum loss that might occur within a certain confidence interval (i.e., within a specified probability limit). VaR does not inform as to the maximum possible loss but only that there is a certain probability that losses will exceed a specified amount. For example, a VaR of US$1 million with a 95 percent confidence interval means that a 5 percent probability exists that losses will exceed US$1 million or, equivalently, a 95 percent probability exists that losses will be less than US$1 million. If we consider a one-day horizon, it means that, on average, every 100 days losses will exceed US$1 million in 5 of those days. VaR does not specify, however, the amount of possible losses outside of the confidence interval.

[15]Artzner, Delbaen, Eber, and Heath (1999) developed four desirable properties that any proposed measure of risk should satisfy. If these four properties are satisfied by a proposed risk measure, then that risk measure is said to be a *coherent risk measure*. One of the properties is subadditivity, the property that VaR does not have, and therefore, VaR is not a coherent risk measure.

Another source said, "We use VaR as part of the asset/liability management [ALM] study to determine strategic asset allocation. We have not found anything much better. VaR is only so useful. It gives a 95 percent confidence level, but as in 2008, people forget to look at the remaining 5 percent. If one wants to cover the 5 percent or even 1 percent, the black swan events, you might as well become an insurance firm that gets by with 2 or 3 percent returns."

Sources agreed that even if properly measured, risk was not always properly considered because the focus was on returns. The CIO of a Dutch industrywide pension fund said,

> We use VaR and saw in the calculation results that there was a high level of risk. We saw the risk on paper but failed to take it into consideration. We run VaR calculations weekly, monthly, but the results were not included in management reports. Risk was shown in strategic papers that the board did not see. In the future, we need to look at risk better, much better. In the past, the policy was you can only control risk. What mattered most were returns, and then next, we looked at the risk. We need to turn this upside down, to look at the risk first and ask, Can we live with this risk and accept the returns?

The CIO of a large public-sector pension fund added,

> Certainly it was foolish to focus solely on VaR, to forget that life has fat tails, that there is kurtosis,[16] that there are inevitable surprises. Could we have been less surprised by events? Risk models are not as robust as they could be. Only in the last five years has the investment management industry put considerable investment into risk management, and we still do not have the tools to manage risk on the private side. In addition, the more we create tranches, the more difficult it becomes; there are tremendous risks at the agency level.

The source added, "We tracked VaR throughout the crisis but did not use it as our main measure. Rather, we used correlations. Our risk management is driven by factors."

Beyond VaR

A fundamental critique of VaR was made by the CIO at a U.K. asset management firm. The source suggested using conditional VaR (CVaR) and looking at the system as a whole. An extension of VaR, CVaR extends the scope of the risk assessment to the tail end of the distribution of losses. Unlike VaR, CVaR is

---

[16]Kurtosis refers to the peakedness of a probability distribution and is the so-called fourth moment of a probability distribution. From a risk perspective, the larger the kurtosis of a probability distribution relative to the kurtosis of the normal distribution (which is 3), the greater the tail risk. The difference between the kurtosis of a probability distribution under consideration and that of the normal probability distribution is referred to as "excess kurtosis."

subadditive and allows investors to aggregate the risk of more than one portfolio.[17] According to this source, "There has been an overdependence on VaR along with a lamentable lack of understanding on the part of users. We use conditional VaR systematically to capture third- and fourth-order moments. We have found that CVaR can be explained reasonably well to clients if done pictorially."[18]

The CIO at a Dutch industrywide fund agreed. This source said, "Given recent market turbulence, we have been looking at new ways to measure risk. CVaR seems promising. Results can be presented to the trustees and understood. We have begun to experiment with CVaR and expect that as of 2010, we will be using the measure as a matter of course."

Among sources that mentioned that they were either already using or currently evaluating the use of risk measures other then VaR, CVaR was the most frequently cited methodology. Other methodologies include Monte Carlo simulations (for the ability to model different scenarios), stress testing (to test assumptions under different hypothetical market conditions), and extreme value theory (to compute the distribution of the maximum value of losses).

The CIO at a Scandinavian buffer fund said,

> Risk management is the area that has changed the most since the events of mid-2007 through 2008. We are using new models. We use VaR and Monte Carlo simulations and are beginning to understand the concepts, the measures of CVaR, and extreme value theory. New models are always the starting point. But you need to see the evolution of risk, the discipline of running the numbers through your head to understand what the numbers mean. The problem is that risk models are based on historical data. We need to explore both shorter and longer periods. In the past, we looked at the next 18–24 months. Now we need to look at different time horizons, from three months to longer, such as three and five years.

One consultant remarked, "We do stress testing to shock the assumptions on which asset allocation is based. What if the assumptions don't hold? For example, we consider real estate and other asset classes and push the correlations to 0.9. People can understand stress testing. We show the possibility of outcomes and shock the decision makers to experience what would happen if assumptions do not hold."

The CIO at a large Scandinavian pension fund suggested, "We should be thinking along the lines of factor analysis—for example, the shock on a portfolio of interest rate risk (our pensions are indexed) or the portfolio's liquidity: What kind

---

[17]Although there are often slight nuances in definitions, CVaR is also referred to as mean shortfall risk, tail VaR, and average VaR. Because CVaR is subadditive and it satisfies the other three desirable properties of risk measures set forth by Artzner, Delbaen, Eber, and Heath (1999), it is a coherent risk measure. Rockafellar and Uryasev (2000) demonstrated that CVaR is a coherent risk measure.
[18]One of the major advantages often cited by advocates of VaR is that it is a concept that can be understood easily by clients.

of liquidity might we need? We are seeing billions of dollars of swings in a day. This volatility has led us to expand arrangements with banks, for example, to increase the liquidity in portfolios."

Extreme value theory (EVT) studies the behavior of extreme (i.e., tail) events.[19] Although few organizations regularly use EVT in risk management (it is considered to be a difficult measure to communicate), some are considering adopting the methodology. The CIO at a fund in central Europe said, "All risk models depend on data from the past. Event risk is not embedded in these models. We are now looking at extreme value theory, fat-tailed risks. EVT helps in reasoning, but the problem remains in that we have to make decisions under uncertain conditions."

A source that is using CVaR among other risk measurement methodologies suggested that this approach is not enough. According to this source, "Even CVaR does not tell us what the maximum loss might be. We need to look at the system as a whole, the macro links. A macro view is very useful. We ask our macroeconomists not only to give their views on inflation, GDP, and so on, but for more of a strategic, operative view as all volatilities and correlations are going up."

Systemic risk was singled out as a key challenge in risk management; addressing the challenge will require a better understanding of macroeconomic phenomena and their relationship to financial markets. As things stand today, the tools for measuring systemic risk do not exist. It is an area of research. One consideration is the need to recognize that the economy is finite, with finite resources. The need to recognize the finiteness of markets was cited by several sources.

Funding Ratio

For institutional investors, the biggest risk is the risk of not being able to meet liabilities. This concern has led institutional investors and their consultants to focus on the funding ratio. As mentioned earlier, it has been estimated that by year-end 2008, the financial crisis had wiped out more than 20 percent of the value of managed assets at U.S. pension funds, life insurance companies, endowments, foundations, and mutual funds, thus causing severe underfunding at many defined-benefit pension funds.

A source at a corporate pension fund in Europe said, "The most important measure is the funding ratio. The plan sponsor is a listed firm. By Belgian law, pension plans must be 100 percent funded. Our objective is to not need to go to the plan sponsor to ask for more money."

If the investment process is based on establishing benchmarks for each mandate to run a part of the fund's money, risk is defined as the risk of underperformance relative to a benchmark and is measured as tracking error. Sources are generally

---

[19]For a further discussion of extreme value theory, see Embrechts, Klüppelberg, and Mikosch (1997).

satisfied with the state of performance measurement, although some think that it has been "dumbed down" as investors have focused increasingly on returns in recent years.

One of these, a source at a large U.S. consultancy, said,

> Today's methods of performance evaluation are rather crude. Starting in the late 1960s, there was a wealth of information on performance measurement and new techniques and more refined methodologies, including risk-adjusted performance measures. The fact is that most fund supervisors are not interested in more refined measures. The old idea of comparing performance to a benchmark persists. Actual decision making is based on net returns compared to a benchmark without adjustment for risk. Performance reports today consist of just a page of numbers with rates of return. Endowments led the way. They considered that there were more important things to do than to calculate risk-adjusted returns. The idea was that the real work was in manager selection and that there was too much noise around performance. Institutional investors today are asking only, What was the fund return benchmark and did the manager beat it or not? A lot of measurement stuff is considered a fine point; institutional investors want only raw numbers.

Still, another consultant commented, "What has been successful has been to move away from a benchmark approach to look at the funding level and the risk in relation to the funding level. It is not a question of how frequently you look at risk but how risk is broken down, how it is measured in relation to the funding level. For example, looking at performance relative to a benchmark when the manager outperformed by 2 percent but the benchmark was down 20 percent is not useful."

A consultant in the United States asked, "Are our methods adequate? We do measure the higher moments of distributions and some tail risk. Plan sponsors are asking what such an event would mean to their plan. We need to think more about more conservative portfolios. Plan sponsors are having more and more frequent conversations about risk and tail events. Rather than focus on a specific measure, we suggest that plan sponsors look at the expected long-run costs to meet obligations instead of looking at the funding ratio."

Product Innovation and Risk

Some sources blamed excessive financial innovation for the most recent financial crisis. A European asset manager said that investment banks are responsible for having introduced risk into the market. According to this source, "Investment banks conducted business in a way that indicates they were not looking for a fair distribution of risk in the market, with their packaging and repackaging things."

The CIO at a North American public-sector fund agreed,

> Bankers wanted to make too much money and were securitizing everything. Those who measured market risk and credit risk did so properly. The issue was that they were not able to see through the structures they were investing in. Investors did not see the extent of leverage in the system. You can make use of all the measures you

like, but you need to understand what you are investing in. Lots of people were measuring risk but did not understand what they had invested in—the leverage. Risk measures, such as VaR, have taken a hit, but the problem was not the tools; you need a broader understanding of risk than can be achieved with just one number.

In addition to investors not understanding the products they were buying, there was a lack of sufficient history available to investors on these products. One source said, "There is nothing wrong with the risk measures that we use, but the way that we use them is problematic. For example, consider mortgage-backed securities. People used the history of prices that went back five years, but there was no shock during the last five-year period. Here is where the role of the macroeconomist or the macro analyst comes in, to look into product innovation and the risk on the macro and micro level."

Explaining Risk to the Investor

Investors, be they institutional, high-net-worth, or retail, were largely caught off guard by the 2008 market crash. To a certain extent, this might be surprising, given that investors have been told that there is no free lunch, that risk is their only asset. An asset manager in the United States said, "Never underestimate greed, in the broadest sense of the term; the power of capitalism to reward risk taking is good, but people's behavior is not necessarily self-moderating. It has led to trouble, to lax lending, and to lax underwriting standards. It makes it easy to make money. When things go wrong, really wrong, just about everyone is complicit."

For some institutional investors, the problem was reducing the contribution of the plan sponsor, paying the pension promise, or simply maximizing returns, so risk was put on the table. One investment consultant remarked, "Risk management has been heavily criticized, and risk tools have been heavily criticized. But there is a misconception; financial market returns are not normally distributed. If you give the investor a richer set of figures, for example, do stress testing or use CVaR, it is not always helpful in decision making because the investor might see too much risk in a one-year period. If you use all these measures to determine the risk budget, it might result in too conservative an asset allocation."

The CIO of a Swedish buffer fund suggested that investors need to reduce their expectations. He commented, "What returns are they counting on for the future? Seven percent? But that is like being on artificial breathing, with money being pumped into the system. With innovation, you will get some growth, but it is questionable that growth will be as high as it has been. We need to lower return expectations. We are working on the hypothesis of 4 percent real return, but we need to understand that there will be periods when returns will be lower and periods when they will be higher."

As for the retail investor, as one source remarked in Chapter 2, he or she typically fails to separate manager returns from market returns. A misalignment of expectations and reality exists. Asset managers do not *produce* returns in the same way that a company produces an industrial product. As an industry, asset managers can optimize the choice of investments for their clients. Although such an approach may be less remunerative, sources mentioned that investors are no longer willing to pay 2 percent management fees. As a matter of fact, investors are increasingly putting their money in low-cost funds. The *2009 Investment Company Factbook* (Investment Company Institute 2009) reported that all net new cash flows to U.S. stock funds during the 10-year period of 1999–2008 went to funds with below-average expense ratios (see Chapter 4). An asset manager in France said, "As an industry, it is true that we do not produce alpha; our role is one of transformation. We add value by transforming risk."

A source in Germany added,

We have learned several things from the crash of 2008. One thing pertains to selecting funds for the private investor. We have learned that whole market segments can become totally illiquid, so one has to be more careful in selecting instruments for funds. Another thing we have learned is the need for better communication with the investor in regards to risk and opportunities, especially in regards to equity funds. Managers should advise the investor not to put his or her money in equities unless the time horizon is long, more than 10 years.

Even 10 years might not be a sufficiently long time horizon. The first decade of the 21st century has been described as a lost decade for equities. During the 10-year period ending year-end 2009, the Dow Jones Industrial Average (DJIA) was down more than 9 percent from January 2000; the S&P 500 was down more than 24 percent; the NASDAQ was down more than 44 percent; the U.K. FTSE All-Share Index was down 16.9 percent; the FTSEurofirst Index was down 29.6 percent; and the Tokyo Stock Price Index (TOPIX) was down 47 percent. The importance of the timing of an asset allocation decision was underlined in conversations with sources.

At the European Union level, regulators are deliberating about how to better protect the retail investor. An industry observer remarked, "The biggest change occurred in 2007 when European directives came into effect making it mandatory to give judicious advice to investors. The Committee of European Securities Regulators [CESR] is now deliberating on the idea of a synthetic indicator of risk for labeling retail investment products."

Some plan sponsors are redesigning their defined-contribution (DC) plans, not removing risk entirely but seeking to reduce it. A source in the United States that is redesigning its DC plan said, "We are creating a default plan that will allow plan members to replace a defined-contribution pension by using a sort of annuity-like income-management option based on an insurer instrument. It will not offer a guarantee on the principal but a guaranteed lifetime withdrawal benefit calculated as a percentage of income on a high-water mark."

As for high-net-worth (HNW) individuals, sources mentioned that risk awareness is low. An adviser to the affluent remarked, "Private investors typically do not know the sources or the measures of risk." HNW individuals see risk more in terms of whom they are doing business with (i.e., counterparty risk). A source at a private bank said that clients now want to know who their counterparty is at both the product and bank level; they also typically check the bank's legal structure, investor protection, and financial strength.

Learning from the Past

What is the next risk that will catch investors off guard? The CIO at a Swedish buffer fund said, "We can already see that people are again doing the same thing at the same time. People are now [3Q09] behaving like lemmings, all running with the same ideas. Everyone is getting into Asian shares. Whatever comes out as a new idea is on everyone's lips, leading to herding, which will hurt performance in the end." A U.K. asset manager added, "There will be product innovation. The problem is that everyone is likely to be herding into the last best thing." We will have to wait awhile to see what that was.

4. Cutting Management Fees and Other Costs

"If returns are low, the cost of producing them becomes more and more important," one source commented. Losses incurred by investors since the markets peaked in 2007 have increased the sensitivity of institutional, high-net-worth, and retail investors to management costs. We will first look at recent trends in management fees and then discuss what investors are doing to reduce fees.

Trends in Management Fees

Investment consultants we talked to remarked that a substantial inflation of management fees has occurred over the years. In a recent note to clients, Towers Watson's Craig Baker (2008) emphasized just how much fees have grown. According to the London-based investment consultancy, by 2008 fees were up about 50 percent compared with 2002, going from 65 bps annually for large funds to 110 bps when the note was published in February 2008. One reason fees were up was investors' appetite for alternatives. Although annual fees charged for traditional long-only active management were often less than 50 bps, Baker calculated that, on a gross annualized return of 15 percent, an investor in a hedge fund would pay the manager 65 percent of the alpha produced and, if the investment went through a fund of hedge funds, the investor would pay 95 percent of the alpha in fees. Calculations run for private equity funds and funds of private equity funds gave similar results. Baker's note also highlighted the fact that active equity managers were being paid "alpha fees" for "beta performance" because the main driver of returns in the bull market from 2003 to 2007 was the strength of the markets.

Based on its data, Towers Watson (2008) examined the entire fund food chain, including not only manager fees but also fees of consultants, custodians, and performance measurers, as well as transaction costs. It found that the total cost rose more than 50 percent between 2002 and 2007, from 63 bps to around 119 bps (see **Figure 4.1**).

Towers Watson's pension fund food chain refers to all the costs incurred by funds in managing their investments. These costs include fees to their investment managers, consultants, custodians, and performance measurers, as well as transaction costs (brokerage commissions, bid–offer spread, taxes, and other costs). As Figure 4.1 shows, Towers Watson estimates that the costs in this food chain have risen globally by more than 50 percent between 2002 and 2007 to around 119 bps per year. It attributes the increase largely to higher investment management fees and transaction costs as funds have raised their exposure to more expensive alternative asset classes. In contrast, Towers Watson finds that funds typically spend little on internal resources (it estimates this expense to be around 5–10 bps).

Figure 4.1. Towers Watson's Pension Fund Food Chain

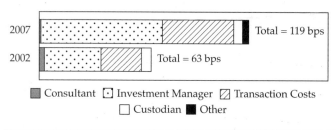

Note: 2002 and 2007 calculations contain methodological differences.
Source: Based on data from Towers Watson (2008, p. 12).

Richard Ennis (2005) commented on the upward trend in active management fees in the article "Are Active Management Fees Too High?" Writing back in 2005, Ennis remarked that although indications were that over the past 30 years it had become harder, not easier, to beat the market, the price of active investment products had been rising steadily. Using figures from Lipper, a Thomson Reuters company, he noted that the average equity mutual fund expense ratio had risen from 0.96 percent in 1980 to 1.56 percent in 2004 (see **Figure 4.2**).[20]

Figure 4.2. Average Equity Fund Expense Ratio (equal weighted), 1980–2004

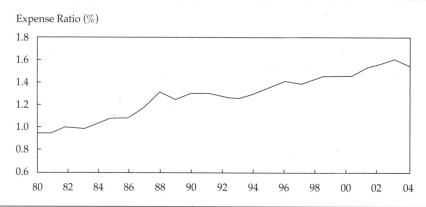

Note: Data are from Lipper, a Thomson Reuters company.
Source: Based on Ennis (2005, p. 46).

[20] As investment continues to flow to lower-cost funds, the weighted average expense ratio of mutual funds has recently declined even more. According to Lipper, the total expense ratio for open-ended mutual funds in 2008 was 1.18 percent.

Ennis wrote, "Just as striking is the fact that a price increase of this magnitude would occur while revenues soared in an industry characterized by ease of entry and minuscule marginal costs."[21] He cited figures from UBS Global Asset Management that show the value of assets available to be managed in capital markets worldwide grew from US$7.5 trillion in 1980 to US$87.2 trillion by 2004. Ennis calculated that the higher the price of investment management, all else being the same, the harder it is to deliver the investor a *net* gain from active management (see **Table 4.1**).

Table 4.1. Likelihood of Success under Various Fee Rates

Fee	Manager Skill Required for Investor to Have at Least a 50/50 Chance of Earning a Positive Alpha	Investor's Probability of Earning a Positive Alpha When Manager Skill Is 0.80
0.5%	0.62	0.70
1.5	0.83	0.46
3.0	0.97	0.15

Note: Ennis's measure of manager skill is the *ex ante* probability that a manager will produce a positive cumulative alpha, after transaction costs but before management fees, over the course of 10 years.

Source: Ennis (2005, p. 47).

Investors are taking various steps to rein in management fees. We will talk about the response of institutional and high-net-worth individual investors and then of retail investors.

Renegotiating Management Fees

Institutional investors who watched their assets shrink as equity markets lost around half of their value during the last market crash are now reexamining management fees and other costs. They are responding by renegotiating fees, moving more assets into passive investments, bringing management (increasingly) in-house—including setting up in-house teams in the alternatives arena—and pooling assets to wring out layers of intermediaries. Obviously, the latter strategies are open only to the larger institutional investors.

---

[21]Jefferies & Company, Inc. (2007), calculated the industry's physical capital requirement (excluding compensation) to be roughly US$200,000 to US$400,000 per US$1 billion managed and to drop dramatically as asset levels rise above US$1 billion. It remarked that additional business yields high marginal profits.

Forty percent of the institutional investors with €207 billion in investable assets as well as nearly all the investment consultants reported that they were actively trying to decrease management fees. One way to reduce fees is to renegotiate with external managers. Although the need to reduce fees is particularly felt in the alternatives arena, sources are also working to bring down the cost of traditional asset management, despite it being reportedly less elastic.

Indeed, our sources had mixed opinions about the possibility of reducing management fees at traditional managers. An investment consultant in northern Europe said that his firm has seen fees for traditional management fall by 10–15 percent. But a source at a large private pension fund in the same country, speaking at the end of summer 2009, remarked, "While we will negotiate fees down for hedge funds, it is more difficult to do so for traditional managers. The question for the latter is, Can they stay alive when their asset base has dropped so much? Traditional managers are at a critical point and cannot afford to drop their fees."

Sources in the United Kingdom are also divided about the possibility of negotiating a decrease in management fees at traditional asset management firms. Some said they had successfully negotiated fees down by 10–20 percent on active equity and bond portfolios; others reported that traditional fund managers are not reducing fees. A U.K. consultant remarked, "There is definitely a lot more flexibility than there used to be, but the ability to negotiate management fees down depends on the mandate. We encourage clients to be cost conscious and take a share of the savings, be it in custody costs, asset manager fees, or other."

The head of one of the biggest asset management firms in the United Kingdom agreed that more flexibility exists now in negotiating fees but thinks the room for negotiation is limited. According to this source,

> Investment management seems to be insensitive on price except in passive management. In active management, there is a standard fee and not much evidence that it is falling. I expect it to hold. Even if investors say that they can negotiate down 10–15 percent, that is not much of a reduction. It used to be that investors would talk with the asset manager, and the manager would say, "This is my fee." Investors would try to negotiate but the asset manager would say, "Take it or leave it." In the end, investors accepted the fee. The same process is happening now, but the asset manager agrees to negotiate downward 10–15 percent. That is not a big repricing of the industry.

In North America, the CIO of a large pension fund that is aggressively renegotiating management fees and trying to reduce costs because assets are down remarked, "We are looking at portfolios on a cost basis. Our objective is to reduce external management costs by 15 percent. It will not be easy, and we will not get there with all managers, but by renegotiating with both traditional and alternative managers, we hope to achieve our objective."

Interestingly, even before the market turmoil that started in mid-2007, investors were shifting assets under active management from expensive to lower-cost products. Ennis (2005) cited data from the Simfund mutual fund database of Strategic Insight, an Asset International Company, which shows that during 1999–2004 investors increasingly favored lower-cost managers (see **Table 4.2**). Ennis wrote, "[Table 4.2 shows that] in 1999, funds in the top two quintiles [sorted by expense ratio (ER)] took in US$46 billion in net cash inflows; the bottom two quintiles took in US$30 billion. In 2001, a shift occurred: The top two quintiles had net cash *outflows* of US$6 billion, whereas the two lowest had *inflows* of US$10 billion. In 2002, all flows were outflows. Years 2003 and 2004 are similar to one another in that the two most expensive quintiles experienced sizable net cash outflows whereas the least expensive garnered even larger net inflows."

Table 4.2. Net Cash Flows to Active Large-Cap Domestic Equity Mutual Funds ($ billions)

ER Quintile	Typical ER Range	1999	2000	2001	2002	2003	2004
1 (highest)	>2.00%	$21.1	$16.4	−$4.4	−$ 8.3	−$ 4.4	−$ 6.2
2	1.61–2.00	25.0	13.0	−1.3	−17.9	−8.0	−11.7
3	1.26–1.60	3.2	0.3	−2.5	−5.9	4.6	2.1
4	1.00–1.25	0.4	11.2	5.7	−4.9	0.2	0.2
5 (lowest)	<1.00	29.8	−1.3	4.7	−0.3	32.0	28.4
Total net flow		$79.5	$39.6	$2.2	−$37.3	$24.4	$12.8

Note: Data are from the Simfund mutual fund database of Strategic Insight Mutual Fund Research and Consulting.

Source: Based on Ennis (2005, p. 48).

As mentioned earlier, much of the reduction of fees realized has been in the alternatives arena. A U.K. consultant commented, "The interesting thing is that investors now have the power to negotiate better terms, especially in alternatives." In addition to trying to reduce fees, many sources said they are also trying to extend the time period used to determine performance fees to multiple years instead of one year. The CIO at a large Scandinavian fund that is flexing its muscles said,

We can now push much more for lower fees because capital is scarce. But it depends on the asset class. In passive equities, one might be able to gain a few basis points, but in private equity, one can negotiate fees down by 25–40 percent. Pension funds have the capital that managers now need. It was easier for private equity to discuss terms with high-net-worth individuals than with public pension funds. But as high-net-worth individuals have pulled their money out, private equity firms are forced to turn to public pension funds, which need to get skillful [management firms] at a fair price.

As for hedge funds, a source in the United States remarked, "The fee structure will continue to resemble what we know today, but base fees will come down from 2 percent to 1.5 percent or 1 percent. Plus, we will see some drop in performance-based fees." A similar fall in fees was noted by a source at a large pension fund in the Benelux region (Belgium, the Netherlands, and Luxembourg), which saw its fixed management costs at hedge funds drop to 1.5 percent from 2 percent while performance fees dropped to 15 percent from 20 percent. In addition, this large institutional investor is negotiating to move performance fees to a multiple-year period from the one-year model.

Although sources commented that fees at poorly performing funds in the alternatives space were down even more than 20–30 percent in 2009 compared with 2008, some sources questioned if it is even worthwhile to negotiate a decrease in fees with nonperforming funds. One source said, "In alternatives, there is scope for cost cutting, especially in hedge funds and private equity. But one must ask, 'Do I want to be with a hedge fund that has not done well in the recent crisis with a lower fee or simply say good-bye?'"

Another strategy investors are using to reduce costs in alternatives is to get out of funds of funds. A Swiss investment consultant remarked, "Investors are getting fees down by cutting their investments in funds of hedge funds, thereby reducing the double level of fees."

Rather than putting the emphasis on costs, however, some institutional investors are putting the emphasis on the need for a better alignment of the interests of managers and investors.

The managing director of a €2.5 billion pension fund in central Europe said, "Cost is not the first issue on our list because there is no advantage if you pay less and receive less. The need is to make sure that the incentive scheme at an asset management firm is right—for example, that it does not encourage the manager to take on more risk for a short period of time. When looking at external managers, we want to understand how their incentive system works."

Chief executives of U.K. asset management companies have apparently also heard the message. A survey of 30 CEOs at traditional and hedge fund management companies conducted by the U.K. consultancy Investit found that agreement exists on the need to change the remuneration and fee structures used by the industry, aligning the latter more closely with the investors' interests (Investment & Pensions Europe 2009c).

Even the very wealthy, sources reported, are trying to get management fees down. According to one source that advises high-net-worth individuals in Switzerland, "Clients are asking themselves how they can make up the revenues loss. They are moving toward simpler, more transparent products, such as exchange-traded funds [ETFs]. The whole issue of hidden fees and kickbacks has come under pressure. Traditionally, pressure on revenues was not so high (in wealth management), but now there is less of a distinction between on- and offshore revenues for wealth managers."

Another source that also advises high-net-worth individuals in Switzerland said,

Costs are now the center of investors' attention. When performance is down, the manager might blame it on the market, but when clients look at their fee statements, they get very nervous. There is now more talk about costs and fees. But we are not seeing high-net-worth individuals renegotiating fees downward. What is happening more often is that investors leave their old adviser, go to a new bank, and find that they are offered more competitive fees—excluding the hidden costs. Fees for private wealth management have dropped from 1.2–1.5 percent of assets under management to 1 percent or less.

A study by Binder and Nolterieke (2009) of MyPrivateBanking.com that included the 20 biggest European private banks with offices in Switzerland found that half of the banks indicated a willingness to reduce their list price without being asked to do so.

In another paper, Nolterieke (2009) considered a US$1 million balanced portfolio invested 40 percent in stocks, 40 percent in bonds, 10 percent in hedge funds, and 10 percent in cash. In addition to a direct management fee of 0.8 percent plus transaction fees calculated at 1.0 percent per trade, Nolterieke calculated the hidden costs for different investment products. For example, he calculated that the hidden yearly management fee for a US$100,000 investment in ETFs is 0.3 percent; for a US$400,000 investment in actively managed equity or bond funds, the hidden yearly management fee is 2 percent; and for a US$100,000 investment in hedge funds, the hidden yearly management fee is 4 percent (see **Table 4.3**).

Sources at private banks agreed that margins are coming under pressure. A source in Geneva said, "As always, private investors are more sensitive to costs with markets going down, although the pressure has lessened in the past months as financial markets rebound. While the official fee structure has not changed, it is difficult to refuse to review up-front fees when investors lost 30 percent in one year. We are now negotiating up-front fees down 10 to 20 percent."

Looking for Additional Savings

Sources reported that institutional investors are also looking to cut costs in areas other than management fees, such as trading costs. One investment consultant said, "While I do not see management fees coming down yet, the expectation is that the greater transparency that new regulation will bring will force fees down on less-value-added operations. There will be more focus on the transparency of costs and the breakdown of costs—for example, looking at commissions, trading costs, what managers are earning at what level, and so on."

Table 4.3. Calculated Hidden Costs for Different Investment Products in a Typical Portfolio Held by a High-Net-Worth Investor

Pricing Model	Investment (US$)		Fees[a]		Total Direct Cost (US$)
Management fee	1,000,000	×	0.8% per year (p.a.)	=	8,000
Transaction fee	750,000 trade volume	×	1.0% per trade	=	7,500
Total direct costs of portfolio					15,500

Investment Product	Investment (US$)		Fees p.a.[a]		Total Hidden Costs (US$)
Funds (stocks and bonds)	400,000	×	2.0%	=	8,000
Structured products	200,000	×	2.0%	=	4,000
Hedge funds	100,000	×	4.0%	=	4,000
ETFs	100,000	×	0.3%	=	300
Single stocks and bonds	100,000	×	0.0%	=	0
Cash	100,000	×	0.0%	=	0
Total hidden costs of portfolio					16,300
Total costs of wealth management					31,800 = 3.2% p.a.

Note: US$1 million investment: balanced portfolio (stocks 40%/bonds 40%/hedge funds 10%/cash 10%).
[a]Average fees: Other hidden costs like spreads and front loads are not included.
Source: Based on data from Nolterieke (2009, p. 9) and MyPrivateBanking.com.

The director of investments at a large Dutch fund said, "There is now the possibility to bring down costs, and we expect to renegotiate on costs. It is always easy to bring down the low-hanging costs, but we have undertaken a study to understand where the costs are, who is influencing them, and who is behind them in order to have a more specific target."

Trading costs are one obvious place to start. The CIO at a large Scandinavian fund said,

> Trading costs are only a fraction of the cost of managing assets, but our culture is to reduce costs; we are managing other people's money and should not pay too much. We use direct market access [DMA] for execution and are doing more and more of our own execution. We are also being opportunistic in using the present environment to reduce costs. We have a strength, capital, and now is the time to use it. We are using an investment bank's platform and have reduced commissions. Instead of paying the bank 10 bps, we have reduced the amount by several basis points. We are trying to unbundle commissions and are having discussions with investment banks about what is a fair price.

A consultant in the United Kingdom added, "There are two parts to trading costs: (1) the charges—that is, the fee the trader pays the broker—and (2) the bid–offer spread. The fees are coming down quite significantly. As for the latter, the bid–offer spread has been high recently because volatility has been reduced and trading volumes are down in certain areas, such as swaps."

Performance-Based Fees for Traditional Managers?

Typical in the alternatives space, performance-based fees for traditional managers are being implemented in the Netherlands and Germany and (to a lesser extent) in Switzerland; elsewhere, sources reported that performance-based fees are rare. The rationale for introducing performance-based fees in traditional management is that, as one source put it, "Investors do not want to pay for no performance."

The CIO at a large Scandinavian fund remarked, "The problem is not so much performance-based fees as when managers do not get outperformance. We do not worry about sharing returns but want a low fixed cost. We now use performance-based remuneration with 7–8 percent of our external managers and hope to see this grow."

An investment consultant in the Netherlands whose clients were moving toward a performance-based fee structure explained, "The idea is the following: If performance is flat, managers should be able to cover their costs but no more. Fees above cost will be justified only if managers outperform. Of our clients, 80–90 percent are now combining flat and performance-based fees." However, the source added, "If one is not careful in moving toward a performance-based fee structure, management fees can eat up 50 percent of the outperformance. If you go the way of performance-based fees, you must put strict caps on remuneration, establish high-water marks, and avoid a cascading effect."

An investment consultant in the United Kingdom suggested how outperformance should be calculated: "A first step is to set hurdles such as T-bills or a realistic fixed percentage reflecting the expected long-term beta exposure so that managers collect fees only on the performance above this benchmark rate. Second, performance fees should be calculated on a rolling three-year basis or longer, not on an annual result. Third, base fees should reflect actual costs."

The "IPE European Institutional Asset Management Survey 2009" (Investment & Pensions Europe 2009b) found that although a greater use of performance fees is desired by participants for all asset classes, only 4 percent from among the survey participants paid performance fees for fixed income, equity, and balanced mandates. In contrast, those saying they would ideally like to see performance-based fees were 28 percent for fixed-income mandates, 32 percent for equity mandates, and 36 percent for balanced mandates.

Still, sources, especially in the United States, reported little movement toward performance-based fees for traditional managers. An investment consultant in the United States reported that few of its clients have opted for a performance-based fee. This source explained, "Performance-based fees introduce a moral hazard. They would require safeguards to get the incentive in line and not change the risk appetite of the manager. In theory, performance-based fees are OK; in practice, they add a lot of complications that need to be thought out." Other sources suggested an easier way to reduce management fees is by indexing their assets.

Whether institutional investors choose to cut management fees by putting their assets in indexed funds or by asking for performance-based remuneration to ensure that they do not pay for performance that is not delivered, asset managers face the prospect of, in the one case, reduced revenues and, in the other case, volatility of earnings.

Renegotiating Consultants' Fees

Asset managers are not the only ones feeling pressure from investors to align fees with performance. Consultants remarked that that their fees and performance are also being scrutinized.

A consultant in Germany said, "Here, the investor has always had the choice to have a flat management fee or a performance-based fee. What is newer is that investors are now negotiating with the consultants for a performance-based fee on the basis of, for example, how successful the consultant has been in picking asset managers that outperform the benchmark. Two years ago, 20 percent of our clients asked for performance-based fees; now 50 percent do."

Elsewhere, however, sources remarked that few clients are asking consultants for performance-based fees: It is simply easier to walk away from the consultant.

Going Passive

As mentioned earlier, another strategy investors are using to reduce fees is to move assets from active to passive management. A U.S. consultant that advises on more than US$800 billion in assets observed that, "Reducing the cost of traditional managers will be achieved by indexing assets." Among the 17 institutional investors that we talked to, almost one fourth of them, cumulatively responsible for managing around €100 billion in assets, said that they had increased the percentage of assets under passive management; none reported a move in the opposite direction.

A consultant in Germany confirmed the shift there: "In general, we have seen a shift from active to passive as it has become clear that after management costs, active has produced no alpha."

The head of pension fund management at a U.K. fund remarked, "We have been moving traditional management more toward passive for the past 12 months. We used to be 40 percent passive but are now 60 percent passive. We have been disappointed with active managers. Passive does follow the market, but active management has not been performing better than passive, and if you add the fees, it is worse."

The CIO of a large Swedish fund said, "Even before the crisis, we went from 50 long-only equity managers to 2 and moved a big part of the actively managed equities into passive. We did this based on an evaluation that the returns generated by active management do not cover management costs."

Sources observed that although passive management's share of the market had been stable throughout the 2002–2007 bull market, the move from active to passive management has accelerated since the market turmoil that started in mid-2007. In a paper on active management fees, Ennis (2005) remarked that although passive management started in the 1970s, it accounted for a negligible percentage of institutional investments before 1980. In the ensuing 25 years, passive management rose to 44 percent of the total domestic equity assets of U.S. pension and endowment funds.

The affluent are also more interested in passive management now. A source advising high-net-worth individuals in Switzerland remarked, "Maybe only 5–10 percent of private wealth investors have an understanding of passive index products. But that 5–10 percent are now pushing their wealth manager on this, and the wealth manager is pushing the portfolio manager. Passive index investments are slowly growing among private wealth investors. It is the future. In Switzerland, we are now seeing a bank run advertising campaigns offering ETFs or passive only to people with US$500,000 to US$10 million to invest!"

Sources at private banks in Switzerland and Luxembourg confirmed that high-net-worth individuals are using ETFs to reduce management costs. A source at a private bank in Luxembourg observed,

> Investors are now aware that there were a lot of hidden fees in such products as funds of hedge funds. They have become more aware of the cost/benefit of these investments. Equity funds in Europe have high management fees—on average, between 1 and 2 percent, even more if you consider total expenses. As high-net-worth individuals get back into equities now that the markets are up, they are doing so using ETFs. Private banks are offering ETFs to their clients even if margins are low because they prefer to keep the client. About 10 percent of client assets are now in ETFs, and I would expect that figure to go to 20 percent within 12 months and then to 30 percent.

Bringing Management In-House

Thirty percent of the institutional investors, managing a total of around €360 billion in assets, said that they will be managing more assets in-house. The CIO at a large northern European fund said, "We are working hard at reducing costs. Currently, 80 percent of our assets are managed in-house, and we intend to grow this slowly."

Institutional investors managing assets in-house typically said they do so for between 11 and 15 bps per year. In addition to cost benefits, sources cited better net performance and better control. Sources at a large North American pension fund said that they decided in 2007 to increase the amount of assets under in-house management from 80 percent of total assets to 85 percent. Reducing costs was one reason, but poor performance from external managers was also cited.

Another institutional investor from North America that presently manages approximately 30 percent of its assets in-house remarked,

> Our motivation for increasing in-house management is net better performance. Not necessarily in passive, as we have estimated that in bringing passive management in-house, we would almost break even relative to the cost of the large index trackers. Rather, we see value in bringing enhanced index and slightly active assets in-house. We have determined that we can do this for one-tenth the cost of an external manager. We are not trying to say that we can do enhanced indexing better than outside managers, but we can use the same models and lower management costs. Our target is 15 bps in costs. While bringing only a small percentage of our assets in enhanced index and slightly active in-house, this represents huge savings in real dollar terms.

Other institutional investors agreed that there are few, if any, cost benefits in bringing U.S. large-cap passive management in-house. The CIO at a large Swedish pension fund said, "We manage passive European equities in-house, but for passive U.S. equities, we use external managers. It's a question of cost; U.S. passive management products are very cheap, only a few basis points. We could try to run this in-house with a few quants, but the savings would not be meaningful."

A source at a large U.K. corporate fund that manages equity assets in-house for an estimated one-tenth the cost of an external manager said, "I estimate that it is beneficial to run assets in-house if a fund has more than £1 billion in assets. But only a minority actually do. What happens is that one year in-house goes horribly wrong, so the trustees decide to outsource and never bring assets back in-house."

In Germany, institutional investors are reportedly bringing in-house the management of fixed income but not equities. Institutional investors in Germany have a total of €120 billion in assets, 85–90 percent of which is invested in bonds (institutional investors are required by law or by policy to generate a return of 3–4 percent annually). A source there said, "The management of bond assets is going in-house. Investors have seen no value added by external asset managers, so they are bringing down the costs by managing the assets internally."

A number of large institutional investors with a total of around €292 billion in assets mentioned that they will be building up their in-house alternatives teams.

A source at a large U.K. corporate fund that manages equity assets in-house said, "We are looking at what skills we should add internally. We have had a private equity team for 10 years and might want to expand its role in, for example, infrastructure, thus creating specialist teams."

The CIO of a Swedish buffer fund observed that the motivation for building in-house teams in alternatives is not only a question of management costs but also of investment risk. This source commented, "As a reaction to high fees, some pension funds are setting up their own hedge funds. But it is not only a question of cost; it is also a question of confidence. What investors have noticed is that a lot of quick-footed money was invested in hedge funds and funds of funds. When the short-term money was withdrawn, the long-term money was hurt."

Cutting Out Layers

Several large industrywide institutional investors mentioned that they will be pooling their assets with the objective, among others, of cutting out intermediaries and thus reducing costs.

A source at a large Scandinavian fund commented, "There is a lot of desire among pension funds to pool assets and do deals directly without involving the sell side. This approach was done to a small extent before the crisis but is now growing. The idea is to pool assets and start a fund. Why? It is a question of cost and confidence, an alignment of interests among the pension funds."

Indeed, the CIO of one of the world's largest pension funds based in northern Europe said in reference to the fund's strategy in alternative markets, "We will be doing a further pooling of assets."

The trend of big pension funds coming together to pool assets is not limited to large players in northern Europe or Canada. A source that advises the industry on products said, "We consult to a lot of big pension funds in Singapore, Queensland, and others in the Far East. These large pension funds are coming together and realizing economies of scale to bring down costs." "However," the source added, "doing something similar in Britain is not possible given the structure of pension funds." Indeed, the average size of a private pension fund in the United Kingdom is much less than £1 billion.

Some funds are big enough to go it alone. Denmark's ATP, one of Europe's largest retirement schemes, with about €85 billion in assets, set up its own venture capital fund in 2006 and, following its success, announced in the fall of 2009 that it was considering starting a second one.

How Retail Investors Are Cutting Management Costs

Although retail investors cannot negotiate their own cost reductions, they can choose what products in which they want to invest. The Investment Company Institute (ICI) reported in its *2009 Investment Company Fact Book* (Investment Company Institute 2009) that more than 100 percent of all new cash flows to U.S. stock funds during 1999–2008 went to funds with below-average expense ratios, whereas, as a group, funds with above-average expense ratios experienced outflows (see **Figure 4.3**). This cash flow was true for both actively managed and mutual index funds.

Figure 4.3.   Percentage of Net Flows to Funds with Below and Above (Simple) Average Expense Ratios

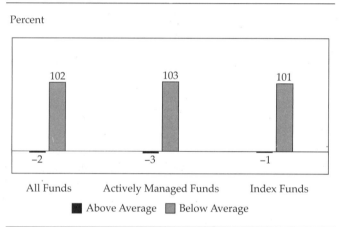

Note: Variable annuities and mutual funds that invest primarily in other mutual funds are excluded.

Source: Based on data from Investment Company Institute (2009, p. 63).

As with institutional investors, private investors are also embracing index funds to reduce fees. According to ICI, of the U.S. households that owned mutual funds in 2008, 30 percent owned at least one index fund. They found that by the end of 2008, a total of US$604 billion was invested in index mutual funds. ICI noted that the share of assets invested in equity index mutual funds relative to all equity mutual fund assets reached 13 percent at the end of 2008, after being stuck between 10.5 and 11.5 percent for the previous six years (see **Figure 4.4**).

Similar cost-sensitive behavior is found among 401(k) plan members. Holden and Hadley (2009) at ICI looked at fees in 401(k) plans, in which 50 million participants had US$2.3 trillion in assets at year-end 2008. The study found that

Figure 4.4. Percentage of Equity Mutual Fund Total Net Assets, 1994–2008

Percent

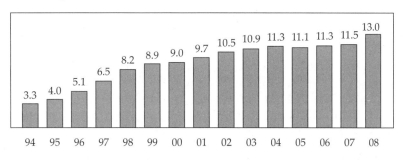

Source: Based on data from Investment Company Institute (2009, pp. 36+).

more than three-quarters of 401(k) stock fund assets was concentrated in funds with expense ratios of less than 1 percent and that almost 30 percent was invested in funds with an expense ratio of less than 0.5 percent, whereas only 3 percent was invested in funds with an expense ratio that was equal to or more than 1.5 percent (see **Figure 4.5**).

Figure 4.5. Percentage of 401(k) Stock Mutual Fund Assets by Expense Ratio, 2008

Percent

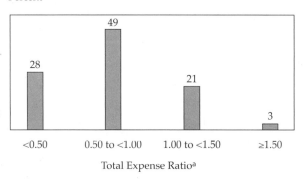

Total Expense Ratio[a]

[a]The total expense ratio, which is reported as a percentage of fund assets, includes mutual fund operating expenses and 12b-1 fee.

Notes: Figures exclude mutual funds available as investment choices in variable annuities. Stock mutual funds include hybrid funds. Percentages do not add to 100 percent because of rounding.

Source: Based on data from Investment Company Institute (2009, p. 14).

Collective investment funds or trusts (CITs), offered by plan sponsors in the United States, are another way small investors are reducing management costs. According to Cerulli Associates, the average total fee on a fund-weighted basis for actively managed CITs with a US$50 million mandate is 71.2 bps, compared with 125–150 bps for an actively managed mutual fund following the same strategy (Glover 2009). SEI Investments Developments (SEI Knowledge Partnership 2008) estimates, however, that the average management fee for a CIT if one looks only at the management fee is equivalent to that of an average institutional large-cap equity mutual fund, which is 0.60 percent. According to SEI, CITs get their price advantage from the regulatory regime that lightens administrative and operational costs. In effect, CITs commingle assets from different accounts into a single fund with a specific investment strategy. Participants own an undivided interest in the aggregate assets of a CIT; they do not directly own any specific asset.

Cerulli estimated that pension funds—defined-benefit and defined-contribution together—held around US$846.2 billion in CITs at the end of the second quarter of 2009. To put this in context, ICI estimated that the U.S. defined-contribution market at year-end 2008 was US$3,500 billion, of which about US$1,500 billion was invested in open-end U.S. mutual funds (Glover 2009).[22]

Although CITs have grown steadily in the U.S. pension market since 2004, as plan sponsors try to reduce plan costs and fees, one source at a U.S. corporate pension fund that has included CITs in its offering said, "Our experience with CITs in 2009 has soured us on this vehicle. You can lose control." This source said that the fund will be moving toward unitized separate accounts.

CITs now have competition from ETFs, which are credited with greater transparency and lower costs. The average expense ratio of an ETF is 0.59 percent, roughly the same as for an average indexed U.S. equity fund.

Pressure to cut management fees for retail investors is also coming in the form of lawsuits brought by investors saying they were overcharged on management fees for retail funds. As of this writing, the Gartenberg standard regarding the establishment of advisory fees and distribution fees is widely applied in the industry in the United States.[23] This standard identifies what are referred to as the "Gartenberg factors" that are considered by advisers and fund trustees in their renewal of the advisory contract. The Gartenberg standard was challenged, however, in *Jones v. Harris Associates*, but the claim was rejected by the United States Court of Appeals for the Seventh Circuit on the basis that fees should be market determined and not established by the courts. In March 2009, the U.S. Supreme Court agreed to review the decision by the lower court challenging the Gartenberg standard in its October 2009 term.

---

[22]For more on CITs, see Comptroller of the Currency (2005).

[23]The 1982 case in which these standards were articulated is *Gartenberg v. Merrill Lynch Asset Management, Inc.*, 528 F. Supp. 1038 (District Court, S.D. New York 1981).

In the United Kingdom, where 8 million people have invested about £450 billion (€482 billion) in defined-contribution plans, the vast majority is invested in low-cost passive equities. The reason is because more than 80 percent of the plan members do not make an active investment choice and thus end up in the default funds, many of which are 100 percent allocated to index-tracking equities (Mannion and Peaple 2009).

At the government level, the objective of a plan to introduce auto-enrollment in the U.K. workplace pension accounts in 2012 is to offer the individual saver low-cost investment products. The plan being debated anticipates an automatic 6–7 percent levy on salaries. The big question, as one source put it, is, What will the money be saved in and who will be managing it? The U.K. government reportedly wants to cap fees at 30–50 bps, including management fees and administrative costs.

5. Moving toward a Redistribution of Roles?

We asked investors, consultants, asset and wealth managers, and industry observers if a redistribution of roles was taking place in investment management. Sources agreed that lines are getting blurred, and the trend toward a greater commingling of roles has accelerated as investors seek ways to protect their invested assets after suffering losses. We will look at how investors are redefining their role and then at how providers of financial services are evolving their service offering. Among the service providers are not only consultants and asset managers but also private banks, investment banks, and insurance companies, coexisting in what Jefferies & Company, Inc. (2007), has called "a clumsy coalition."

Investors: Taking Control of Their (and Third-Party) Assets

Sources observed that large institutional investors and high-net-worth individuals, having been stung by losses in the recent market crash because of asset allocation decisions and being unhappy about paying managers for negative returns, are taking more control of the allocation and/or management of their assets. This move to take more control is coinciding with a growing level of confidence and sophistication on the part of large institutional investors as well as a generational change in wealthy families.

A consultant advising the wealthy in North America and Europe remarked, "Very wealthy families are looking at their aggressive portfolio and noticing that the portfolio is today where it was five years ago. Clients are not happy. They want to get their hands on asset allocation. They will continue to say 'I am not a world expert on this, but if I am going to lose money, I want to know ahead of time and be in control.'"

The desire to be in control is also an objective of institutional investors. A consultant in Germany said, "Many investors have become more professional and are trying to build more resources in-house and not rely solely on outside service providers." The CIO of a US$12 billion corporate pension fund in the United States remarked, "Institutional investors are trying to take back the decisions they own rather than trying to outsource them to others."

A source at a large asset management firm remarked that asset managers rid themselves of the most difficult task in asset management—strategic asset allocation—by pushing it to the end investor, who, ill equipped to handle it, turns to the consultant. According to this source, "Consultants filled this space but have not been able to deal with it. Most consultants are paid on a time charge and cannot compete for talent, given the lower levels of remuneration, yet they have taken on the area of most risk. The general trend now is to move the consultancy business to funds in fiduciary management. Big investors are upscaling their organizations to address the need to do their own strategic asset allocation."

According to press reports, large U.K. corporate pension plans are adding internal investment expertise, including CIOs—a significant move given that the U.K. pension market has been dominated by external advice from investment consultants. The combination of decreased funding ratios and tough financial times brought on by the recent market turbulence has accelerated the move to bring more competence in-house. The head of a London-based consultancy recently told the press, "The amount of news on the collapse of certain markets and supposedly safe instruments has, not surprisingly, increased the fear factor for trustees." According to reports, U.K. pension funds that have recently boosted internal capabilities include the £20 billion Coal Pension Trustees Services, the £17.9 billion Royal Bank of Scotland Group Pension Fund, the £15 billion Barclays Bank U.K. Retirement Fund, the £14 billion Lloyds TSB Group Pension Schemes, the £6.8 billion HBOS Final Salary Pension Scheme, and the £1.6 billion Daily Mail & General Trust Pension Scheme (Carter 2009).

Indeed, all of the large pension funds in North America and Europe with whom we spoke said that they are (increasingly) bringing asset allocation in-house; many are also increasingly bringing the management of assets in-house.

The CIO of one of Europe's largest funds observed,

> The larger, long-term players will be managing their assets in-house. We will see them try to enter the capital markets and bypass both the buy and sell sides—the Goldman Sachs or Morgan Stanleys of this world. We might see the largest 20 or so funds team up with the sovereign funds with whom they have built up a long-term relationship, such as the Norwegian, Australian, or Canadian ones or the French Fonds de Réserve. Large institutional investors have capital at a moment when other players, such as the banks, do not.

The CIO of a Swedish buffer fund concurred: "Pension funds want to pool assets, start a fund, and deal directly without involving the buy or sell sides. This approach was used to a small extent before but is now growing. It's a question of cost and confidence, an alignment of interests among the pension funds."[24]

---

[24]The authors of the "IPE European Institutional Asset Management Survey 2009" found that the share of assets managed internally by 122 responding participants was 41 percent in 2008, up from 32 percent managed internally in 2007. They said that it was impossible to determine if this was the result of a deliberate move by investors, the end result of market adjustments on their portfolios, or a question of a different sampling.

Small funds, however, are generally going another route. A source at a large consulting firm in the United States remarked, "It is not so common here (for a pension fund to bring the management of assets in-house), other than at some large public funds where we have seen some building out of staff. In the private sector, most are trying to minimize their involvement in pension funds." This consultant cautioned, "Many institutional investors are in over their heads: Hiring and setting up an internal organization is one thing; maintaining it is something else."

Similar disengagement among small pension funds is occurring in Europe, where plan sponsors are transferring the management of their pension assets to third parties. One source remarked, "Increased regulation and difficult markets call for more expertise than the average pension fund has. Only the largest pension funds have the requisite skills in-house." In the Netherlands, one source estimated total assets under fiduciary management there at €220 billion.[25]

The larger institutional investors in northern Europe are not only managing more assets in-house, but some are also building up resources, including third-party accounting and administration capability, in an effort to compete with service providers in the fiduciary arena. A source at a large Dutch consultancy observed, "In northern Europe, we are seeing pension funds themselves, such as APG [All Pensions Group], offer asset allocation, asset management, and delivery platforms for third parties. In the Netherlands and Scandinavia, we see three different players: consultants, asset managers, and large pension organizations. They are now on opposite sides of the market, and there is a huge void between them, but all are moving toward the center."

In northern Europe, the expectation is that the trend toward fiduciary management among small funds will benefit the larger ones at the expense of consultants, asset managers, and investment banks. Sources pointed to "very friendly relations" between the large and small Dutch funds. The head of strategy and external management at a large corporate pension fund said, "Here in the Netherlands, fiduciary management is growing and the biggest beneficiaries are a couple of big players—the two big pension funds PGGM and Mn Services, and maybe Stichting Pensioenfonds ABP. All three are well equipped for economies of scale." Nevertheless, while admitting the strengths of these large funds in asset allocation and asset management, some pointed to what they perceive as a weakness of the large funds when competing in the outsourcing market: lack of experience in servicing third parties. Following is the view of an asset manager from the United Kingdom on how fiduciary management will play out in Europe.

---

[25] For more on fiduciary management, see van Nunen (2008).

The trend toward fiduciary management started in the Netherlands. It is now developing in other countries, such as Germany. Fiduciary management calls for a complete practice in asset/liability management (ALM), asset allocation, asset management, liability-driven investment (LDI), insurance, accounting, and administration. The latter two can be done in-house or through third-party providers; the important thing is to maintain control of the whole process. Our choice as a fiduciary manager is to do the accounting in-house but to outsource administration because there are already big players in the market for this function.

Who will be the big players in fiduciary management?

Consulting firms such as Mercer, with what they call implemented consulting. This setup poses a problem in the United Kingdom because investment consultants play such a large role. They have the majority share of the asset allocation role. As an asset manager, we have a number of mandates to manage in a fiduciary role. We are positioning ourselves strongly in the area of fiduciary management but trying not to go against the consultants. The problem is to not engage as an enemy of consultants if you need to gather assets.

Certainly Dutch organizations, such as Mn Services, PGGM, and Cardano [Risk Management BV], are competitors. But it will require a lot of momentum to get the mandates from medium-sized funds. There is the need to overcome language barriers and to win the trust of the board of trustees. The local component is very important. Dutch firms might have a hard time in the United Kingdom and Germany if they do not understand the local needs.

Then there will be stiff competition from the global, international houses. These firms react quickly and have good management tools. BlackRock/BGI, F&C Asset Management, and Goldman Sachs all have made a significant investment in the solutions model. They have the tools, especially the risk management and risk reporting tools, that are essential. The BlackRock/BGI merger is a reflection of what is going on. It will result in a widely expanded product range for the new entity.

Consultants and Asset Managers: Fighting for Turf in Asset Allocation and Asset Management

As we indicated previously, among our sources large institutional investors are taking back ownership of their investment decisions, although sources said that consultants are still being used for such tasks as ALM studies and that, in most cases, at least some assets will continue to be managed externally. As for smaller institutional investors, these will continue to turn to third-party financial service providers for asset allocation, manager selection, and asset management.

We asked sources about their perception regarding a redistribution of roles among consultants and asset managers. A source in the United States summed up the situation: "The neat bins that everyone now sits in will break down. This is happening more in Europe already." Most sources agreed, observing that both consultants and asset managers are trying to carve out new roles for themselves as each tries to reinforce its position with investors who are angry about losses in 2008 and/or to find new sources of revenue. On the one side, consultants are offering implemented consulting (that is, asset management); on the other, asset managers are offering consulting services such as ALM, asset allocation, and even manager selection.

A source at a German consultancy observed, "Investment consultants are increasing their range of services by offering global tactical asset allocation, overlay and hedging techniques, and other services; and asset managers are offering investment-consulting-related services, such as ALM."

The need to increase and stabilize revenue streams was cited as the motivation behind consultants moving into implementation. A source at a large U.S. consultancy said,

> Consultants will be tempted to get more involved in implementation. It is a source of revenue growth for them. What space is opening up? Some funds decided to engage in investing in alternatives and realized that they did not have the resources internally to do so, given the internal staff requirements to run a modern-day investment policy. It does not make sense to add 8, 10, or 12 people. So, consultants offer outsourced discretionary control of the assets. They do not manage the assets directly but have the discretion to move assets and to appoint or fire managers.

A source at a consultancy that acknowledged that fees are under pressure said, "We are more and more involved in implementation. It now represents 50 percent of our revenues. We have always worked this way with family offices and now more with institutional investors. In the mid-1990s, many large universities asked consultants to do hedge fund management. The CIO-outsourcing model started three to four years ago. These developments led to proactive models. This is now the fastest growing part of the consultancy industry."

The need to stabilize (as opposed to increase) revenues was cited as the major factor behind asset managers offering asset allocation advice. A source in the United States remarked, "Asset managers are moving into consultancy not so much as a paid-up business but to offer a new service, information to the client. The accent is not on generating revenues but on building the relationship, offering something over and above just management. There is a need to communicate with the client, to justify fees, especially when performance is down."

If the consulting and management roles converge, as sources, especially those in Europe, widely believe they will, sources think that asset managers have an advantage. A consultant in northern Europe said, "Asset managers will have a slight edge over consultants moving into implementation areas because it is easier for a manager to incorporate asset allocation functions than for a consultant to build an organization to implement strategies."

Nevertheless, sources remarked that asset managers in the United Kingdom are still nervous about stepping into the fiduciary management space because they fear it will damage their relationship with consultants who act as gatekeepers to pension fund assets.

In the United States, sources are more skeptical than their European counterparts about the two roles merging anytime soon. They are also quicker to point to a conflict of interests. A consultant in the United States said, "I have seen no significant redistribution of roles, but different players are stepping into different places: consultants into implementation and discretionary control and asset managers into asset allocation services. There is a blurring of lines, but there is a limit to the blurring. It is hard to merge advice with products or solutions without a conflict of interests."

Not all sources, however, think that the potential conflict of interests, with asset management firms advising on asset allocation and manager selection, is a blocking factor if it is managed carefully. A source at a large corporate pension fund said, "There is no such thing as 'truly independent.' The investor never gets a full range of all possible products, but a narrowed-down choice. The important thing is that the investor is aware of the commercial constraints. If an asset manager assumes the role of manager selection, he or she must have the resources to research other managers."

Some sources pointed to a danger for consultants (or anyone) moving into fiduciary management. One source remarked, "Some consultants are trying to position themselves in implemented consultancy. But there are legal risks involved in this role because they can be sued for not delivering contractual results."

One area in which asset managers are making inroads in asset allocation is in defined-contribution (DC) plans, now estimated to comprise 45 percent of global pension assets. The trend toward default target-date funds in the United States is working in favor of asset managers with global asset allocation models that automatically move in and out of asset classes as objectives and markets change.

A large corporate pension fund in the United States with 42 percent of its pension assets in DC plans is consulting with asset management firms about the structure of its new DC offering, which will include a default fund plus several other choices. The source said, "We are exploring how to redesign our DC plans under the influence of behavioral economists, including elements of target-date funds, the annuity notion, and insurer instruments. In doing so, we are consulting several asset management firms, including AllianceBernstein, Prudential [Financial], Russell Investments, and Wellington Management [Company]."

"Will the asset manager behemoths replace consultants?" one source mused. "BlackRock, GMO [Grantham, Mayo, Van Otterloo & Co.], Wellington, and the like have all-weather portfolios. With their global asset allocation models, they could replace the consultant, but I believe there will always be a need for independent advice."

Even if the two roles do not converge, many investors cited the need for closer cooperation between consultants and asset managers in the area of asset allocation. Not surprisingly, investors who suffered losses as markets plunged in 2008 blamed consultants (at least partially) for poor asset allocation decisions and poor risk management. Many believe that results would have been better if a multiplicity of views had been considered and if consultants had worked closer with those who have experience in running money and with different asset classes.

The CIO at a U.K. pension fund said,

> I expect asset managers and, for corporate sponsors, investment banks to play a bigger role in offering advice to schemes—something similar to the balanced mandates of the 1990s. Balanced mandates were brought down as behind the times and were replaced with specialized mandates. What we are trying to do going forward is get a multiplicity of advice. There is a gray area for investment banks and asset managers in ALM and asset allocation. Both the banks and the asset managers have the computing power and the models.

Asset managers remarked that investors are indeed asking them more frequently for their views on the markets and on asset allocation. A source at a Swiss asset management firm said,

> Previously, if you were a global equity manager, you went to the client and talked about equities. Now, we spend the first 15 minutes talking about our views on various asset classes, protection against drawdowns, return targets, and so on. I expect the role of the consultant to decrease in asset allocation; asset managers will take over some of the issues normally addressed by consultants. If you look back, why do trustees hire a consultant? To enhance the investment but also to protect themselves. But investors experienced losses with the downturn, and investment consultants did not add value on the investment side. Asset managers will play a bigger role in investment decisions.

In all fairness to consultants, sources agreed that asset allocation is harder to get right than stock picking. It must also be said that consultants were not the only ones who failed to foresee the 2008 market crash. As one source observed, "No one called the market crash. It is better not to stick your neck out; there are only downsides to being a Cassandra."[26] For asset managers, taking a bigger role in investment decisions will mean taking back some of the risk of asset allocation. For many firms structured to capture specialized mandates, this addition might require organizational change and new skill sets. One source remarked, "For us, it means we will need the right number of people and the right professional profiles, including good economists on macro and asset allocation issues."

---

[26]Cassandra was the daughter of the Trojan king Priam who had the gift of prophecy but was cursed in that no one would believe her prophecies. In vain, she warned the Trojans against bringing the Trojan horse inside the city walls.

In a recent survey by Investment & Pensions Europe (December 2009), 46 institutional investors in Europe with a combined €454.2 billion in investable assets gave consultants higher marks than they gave asset managers for their asset allocation advice. According to the survey, 20 percent of the respondents rated consultants' asset allocation skills with a score of 9 or 10 out of a possible 10 and 70 percent awarded them a score of 6 or more. Asset managers did not do as well, with less than 8 percent of the respondents awarding them a score of 9 or 10 for asset allocation on the same scale.

Private and Investment Banks: A Bigger Slice of the Asset Management Pie

Private and investment banks are both expected to play a bigger role in some segments of asset management. According to sources, private banks are going onshore and broadening their market by appealing to the mass affluent. Many now base their income on fees, so they are no longer dependent on commissions. This approach allows them to offer such low-cost products as exchange-traded funds (ETFs), to which sources reported the wealthy are turning because of the fees they paid while the value of their assets tumbled in 2008 and early 2009.

An asset manager in Austria said,

> Private banks will be the big winners. They will gain market share. They have already, for the most part, recovered their asset base following the market crash. They are much closer to the investor. And they are enlarging their clientele, now servicing persons with €300,000 to €500,000 of investable assets. These clients are not only buying mutual funds but also ETFs. For a year or two now, private banks have been basing their income on fees for advice. They are no longer dependent on commissions, so they can afford to offer their clients efficient investment vehicles.

The growing role for investment banks in asset management is being driven by institutional investors as defined-benefit pension plan sponsors seek help with funding and immunization. Not surprisingly, the role of investment banks was given the most positive evaluations by sources at private-sector pension plans.

A source at a U.K. pension fund with a multibillion pound deficit remarked, "There will be an increased use of treasury techniques, including such derivatives as swaps and structured products, with increased leverage. Investment banks will continue to increase their presence at the expense of traditional asset managers." Another source in the United Kingdom concurred: "Over the next 10 years, liability-driven investments [LDI], structured products, and swaps will all belong to investment banks."

Nevertheless, consultants, asset managers, and sources at large public-sector or industrywide plans (especially outside of the Anglo-Saxon countries) are more skeptical about the role of investment banks in asset management. They pointed to a transaction-driven mindset and the failure of many structured products to deliver the promised protection.

A U.K. asset manager said, "Investment banks will not be so successful in the LDI market. If a pension fund puts its risk into swaps, an investment bank would see the business as transactional as opposed to relational. If you give an order to Goldman Sachs, there is a question of fair pricing."

The head of a large Dutch industrywide fund said, "Until recent events, investment banks had been increasing their market share with the sophisticated marketing of such products as derivatives. These products were gaining acceptance, but after what happened and the products did not deliver, the market share of investment banks in asset management will shrink."

With reference to the risk in products proffered by the investment banks, a consultant in Germany remarked, "Investment banks should do less marketing and more talking to investors about the risk of their products."

Other sources cited a poor track record in such areas as ALM. A U.K. asset manager said, "Some investment banks got a lot of ALM business because of their big name but then did a poor job. I believe that ALM will be intermediated by the asset manager."

As for the ability of investment banks to grab business in the outsourcing or buyout markets, most sources are skeptical that the investment banks will play a large role. They cited the desire of institutional investors to maintain control of their assets, the dented image of investment banks following recent large losses, and the consequent lack of resources to participate in the buyout market as they rebuild their capital base.

A consultant in Germany remarked, "Investment banks tried to do institutional management, but it was not a success story in Germany. Institutional investors do not want to give away control of the fund. The investment banks wanted to take control of everything, including the discretion to select the asset manager. For the fund, this would be a huge loss of control."

In terms of products at the institutional or retail level, however, sources identified two areas where banks might play a bigger role. One is in the expanding market of ETFs, where investment banks are present with a swap-based product offering. Although some sources expect investment banks to dominate this market within the next 10 years, other sources were quick to point out that a swap-based ETF position does not offer the same institutional safety as one based on a direct investment in the ETF. The collapse of Lehman Brothers in September 2008 exposed the problem of counterparty risk when dealing with entities that were once considered too big to fail.

The other area in which investment banks might play a bigger role is in structured products for the retail investor. This is especially the case in continental Europe, where the investor is conservative and seeks capital protection. A source in Germany said,

The biggest challenge to asset managers has come from the universal banks, especially in the retail sector where they offer certificates (structured products) with capital protection and a share of returns typically in the range of 3–4 percent. Of the certificates sold, 70 percent offer capital protection compared with 5 percent of asset managers' products. Over the past five years, banks have sold hundreds of billions of euros of these certificates. If this competition were not out there, retail fund sales would have been much better.

According to the source, sales of mutual funds in Germany were flat in 2009, after net outflows of €29 billion in 2008. A source in Austria remarked, however, that bank certificates have disappointed, and he believes that the market share of banks in investment products will go down. According to this source,

> Bank certificates were very popular four or five years ago as more and more products were aggressively sold to retail clients via the banks. But now there is a lot of frustration with these structured products. A lot of Lehman certificates were sold; some banks are in trouble, and even if the bank is guaranteed, certificates did not deliver as they were sold to deliver. Clients are disappointed with results. They are now comparing the returns on certificates with normal savings accounts or money market rates.

Following the 2008 market crash and the need to rebuild balance sheets, some banks in continental Europe are reducing their involvement in asset management. In France, Société Générale has transferred its traditional asset management business to rival Crédit Agricole CIB (Corporate and Investment Bank). In Germany, large banks are consolidating and refocusing. A source in Germany remarked,

> Allianz and Commerzbank have done a two-sided deal: Allianz took over Commerzbank's asset management business, and Commerzbank took over Allianz's private banking. The Sparkassen [savings banks] and Landesbanks [public-sector banks with regional ownership] will be consolidating, moving away from investment banking, asset management, and alternatives and back to concentrating on their commercial banking clients—small to medium-sized businesses and individuals. These banks had lost their focus. Some tried to make money with asset management, but the government had to come in and put money back into the institutions to compensate for the mistakes they made. They are now refocusing on their traditional business, loans.

Insurers: A Bigger Slice of the Asset Management Pie?

We also explored the role of insurers in asset management to ascertain whether they were positioned to get a bigger slice of the asset management pie, as some studies have suggested, and how they are positioned. According to sources, the situation varies considerably from country to country.

In the United Kingdom, where a plan to introduce auto-enrollment in workplace pensions is being debated, the government wants to cap fees at about 30–50 bps, inclusive of management fees and administrative costs. It was reported that when government officials were in a room discussing the target levels of remuneration with asset managers and insurance-based pension providers, the asset managers walked out of the room, one after the other, because a typical asset manager's fee for an active equity portfolio is 150 bps. A source reported, "At the end, the only ones left in the room were the big indexers and insurers like the United Kingdom's Prudential and Standard Life. There are a lot of insurers in asset management; they can handle mass savings more cheaply than the asset managers. They also have a retail orientation and better, stronger brands." They also have broader diversification possibilities.

In some countries, insurance firms are benefitting from the move to outsourcing pensions. In November 2009, Finnish State Railways (now VR Group) announced that it was transferring the management of its €471 million in statutory pension liabilities to Varma Mutual Pension Insurance Company, which has €28.3 billion in assets. The State Railway's decision to transfer statutory pension liabilities to an insurer followed recent decisions made by several other Finnish firms and has led some observers to forecast the end of the Finnish corporate pension sector.

In addition, as Baby Boomers retire and switch from accumulating assets in their pension plans to requiring a yield on assets accumulated, the expectation is that in such countries as the United Kingdom and the United States, insurers will play a larger role in managing those assets. In the United Kingdom, the "at retirement" market for annuities—financial products that provide an income until death in return for a large up-front payment—is already estimated to be worth more than £14 billion a year to insurance companies.

In the United States, with an estimated 77 million Baby Boomers headed for retirement, demand for insurance-like products that offer, for example, principal protection and risk mitigation is expected to grow. In looking at the U.S. asset management industry, McKinsey & Company (2006) forecasted that by 2010 investable assets controlled by retirees and near-retirees would represent almost two-thirds of all investable assets. That, according to McKinsey, will fuel the demand for risk-mitigation products to protect against health care risk, longevity risk, market risk, inflation risk, and interest rate risk. McKinsey sees a growing role for insurers and insurance-like products.

In continental Europe, such insurance products as life insurance play a big role in retail investment products. Nevertheless, sources from some countries noted that insurance products have disappointed investors. In an interview conducted in December 2009, a source in Austria who believes insurers' market share in investment products will drop said, "There is a lot of disappointment with life insurers and fund-linked products. Insurers have yet to reveal results, . . . but the numbers are slowly coming out. They were not sufficiently invested in risky assets to get returns."

An often-cited shortcoming of insurers in the investment arena is their relatively low salaries, which is a handicap when trying to compete with asset managers and investment banks for talent. Recent layoffs or hiring freezes by asset managers and other organizations in the financial services sector, however, have allowed insurance firms to recruit talent. In their most recent report on employment trends in asset and wealth management, Russell Reynolds Associates (2009) noted that insurance firms recruited heavily in 2009. According to the report, "Insurance companies were among the most active recruiters (in 2009). Many insurance companies upgraded talent by installing new CEOs for investment subsidiaries, bringing in new CIOs, heads of alternatives, and filling other key roles by taking advantage of access to executives who previously had been difficult to attract." **Exhibit 5.1** summarizes the strengths and weaknesses of banks and insurers in the investment management arena.

Exhibit 5.1. Strengths and Weaknesses of Banks and Insurers in the Investment Management Arena

Type	Strengths	Weaknesses
Private Banks	• Close to the investor • Appeal for the mass affluent • Income that is increasingly based on advice, not commissions, which allows more transparency and freedom to offer low-cost investment products	Positioning that limits clientele to the mass affluent and high-net-worth individuals
Investment/Universal Banks	With corporate plan sponsors: • Established relationship with CFOs • Structuring expertise More in general: • Low-cost swap-based products in exploding ETF market • Risk management • Established distribution network	• Damaged reputations from recent financial crisis • A transactional mentality • Need for liquidity that limits resources for other initiatives • Structured products that do not always deliver
Insurers	• Ability to handle mass savings cheaply • Retail orientation/established distribution network • Strong brands • Longevity/health data and modeling • Risk modeling • Broad diversification possibilities • Ability to provide principal-protection and risk-mitigation products that Baby Boomers entering retirement will require • Ability to spread longevity risk across individuals • Large balance sheets	• Comparatively low returns • Relatively low salaries that make it hard to attract best talent

6. Ethical Dimension

Throughout the second half of 2009, in the wake of the Madoff and Galleon scams, we asked sources if they were more, less, or just as concerned about ethical issues as they had been 12–24 months earlier. Interestingly, European sources typically understood the question to mean the ethics of investment choices whereas U.S. sources interpreted it as the ethics of the manager. We will first look at the latter.

Ethical Dimension of the Manager

Concern regarding the ethics of the manager is not only a question about the safety of one's investment (i.e., will my investment principal be returned) but also a question about less dramatic events, such as insider trading and front running. As for the safety of one's investment, sources in Europe were, in general, confident that the requisite safeguards were in place. A source from Germany commented, "A manager cannot walk away with the money if it is held in a depository bank." But sources agreed that growing investment in hedge funds and in alternatives, where transparency is lacking, has increased the need for more due diligence. As one source said, referring to the post-Madoff world, "Investors are now more aware of the fact that there are unethical people out there."

Sources said that they are dealing with the problem by stepping up their due diligence. Some are implementing "know-your-relations" policies, and others suggested that this situation is another reason to invest in simpler and more transparent structures or to go passive.

A consultant in Germany remarked, "There is a need for more diligence, given greater distrust on the part of the investor. From the point of view of the consultant, this requires much more work when going into a structure that is not 100 percent transparent." A consultant in the United States added,

> In the wake of the Madoff affair and other high-profile investment manager swindles, consultants have come under questioning. As a profession, consultants will need to redouble their efforts to overcome the perception that much of their research is superficial. They will need the wherewithal to perform their duty and build strong research capability, especially in the alternatives area, which will add a cost. Research staff will need to be increased in size and expertise. We now run background checks on managers more often and have a hedge fund research team of 10 persons, one of which is dedicated to operational research. There is the need to demonstrate to investors that one has depth of research and depth of reasoning.

Institutional investors mentioned that as they move into the alternatives space, they are paying more attention to who the other investors are in funds they are considering. The CIO at a large corporate pension fund in the United Kingdom said, "We consider ourselves a long-term investor and want to invest with other long-term investors. We do legal due diligence to make sure that we are protected against hot money coming and going."

The CIO of a Swedish buffer fund concurred: "What people have noticed when discussing hedge funds or funds of funds is that there was a lot of quick-footed money invested in these funds, and when these investors withdrew their money, the long-term money was hurt. Institutional investors will take more time to understand who the co-investors are, especially in funds of hedge funds, now the pariah of the investment community."

Specific to performing due diligence in the alternatives space, the managing director of a large Austrian pension fund chuckled,

> We are happy we did not invest in Madoff's fund. People who were peddling Madoff's fund visited us during 1990–2008. They were trying to sell the product but were unable to explain how returns were obtained. You need to ensure that a strategy that worked in the past will work in the future, take a macro view, do due diligence, and not trust a product just because the person trying to sell it tells you that other important institutions have invested money in the product.

Others remarked that in performing due diligence, it is necessary to go beyond the paperwork. The director of investments at a large Dutch industrywide fund said, "We have learned from the press that there are people that set up Ponzi schemes. We have adopted a new policy: 'Know your relations better, deeper.' We are also paying more attention to gossip."

Since the late 1980s, one of the authors of this monograph has been involved in the performance evaluation of a large number of institutional funds and has participated as a discussant at numerous institutional investor conferences on the issue of performance evaluation. In his view, institutional investors tend to focus on poor-performing managers whereas the focus should be on those managers with outstanding performance that peers cannot approximately replicate.

High-net-worth individuals are also reportedly paying more attention to who is managing their assets. Many suffered losses because their banks had invested in Madoff and/or Galleon funds. A source at a private bank in Luxembourg said, "Clients are now checking who their counterparties are at both the bank and product level. They are running checks on the legal structure, investor protection, quality of the organization, and its financial backing. They want to know who their provider is. Private investors started to look into these things in the 1980s and then let it drop, but now it is back again."

Among the asset managers we talked to, none are positioned completely in the alternatives arena, so they generally reported that they did not have a heightened sensitivity to the ethical dimension of the manager on the part of investors. A source at a traditional management firm that has also developed an alternatives business, however, mentioned that in a difficult situation in which personnel have been laid off and investors are under pressure, it is particularly important to keep a watch for fraud.

Ethical Dimension of Investments

Among consultants and investors, sources in continental Europe agreed that there is more interest in ethical investing compared with 12–18 months ago. A consultant in Germany remarked, "Several years ago, everyone was interested only in performance, not socially responsible investments. Now, the question of ethical investing is becoming more and more important." A colleague in the Netherlands added, "It is hard to imagine that in the future an institutional investor will not be able to answer a journalist's question about, for example, whether he or she is investing in firms that make land mines."

In an effort to make more socially responsible investments, institutional investors in continental Europe are looking more closely at their portfolios. The managing director of a multiemployer pension fund in central Europe said, "We screen the portfolios that managers hold. In the future, we will be looking at their approach to ethical investing, the equity portfolio, the capital evaluation, and what is behind a company's profits, as well as corporate governance issues."

Others, especially institutional investors in northern Europe, consider that they are at the forefront of ethical investing. The CIO of one of the world's largest funds, which manages most assets in-house, said, "We take ethical issues—environmental, social, and governance—very seriously. We have guidelines that are applied to all portfolios; it is not just a question of a specific socially responsible investment portfolio. We have a team of 10 researchers that look after the issue, working together with a third-party service provider that uses text-mining techniques to monitor firms on environmental, social, and governance issues."

The "IPE European Institutional Asset Management Survey" (2009b) also registered a growing interest in socially responsible investing. In Europe, 117 institutional investors with a total of €477 billion in assets participated in the survey. Although almost two-thirds of the respondents reported that they had no plans to increase their socially responsible investing (SRI) or environmental, social, and governance (ESG) assets, SRI/ESG issues were moving up investors' agendas. Social and environmental values were reported to be the number one reason investors have for pursuing these strategies. Interestingly, 8 percent of the investors said that all of their assets were already governed by SRI policy whereas 30 percent said that they were planning to increase their investments in SRI securities (see **Figure 6.1**).

Figure 6.1. European Institutional Investors Planning to Increase Percentage of Assets Governed by SRI Policy in 2010

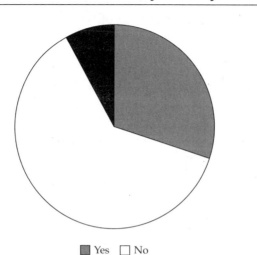

■ Yes ☐ No
■ Already at 100%

Source: Based on data from Investment & Pensions Europe (2009a, p. 38).

Sources in the United Kingdom and the United States, however, typically consider ethical investing an issue only in that it could affect the return on investment. A consultant in the United Kingdom commented,

> Principles in regards to what a fund should or should not invest in are for the investor to determine. We are concerned only when the ethical issues affect the financials—for example, a bad human rights record leads others to pull out their money and the stock price goes down, so it is not a good investment. In the United Kingdom, a legal framework for defined-benefit pension funds includes the formulation of policy on ethical investments. Most funds eschew investments only if the ethical dimension has an implication for the value of the company or the financial outcome.

The CIO of a U.K. pension fund commented, "We take a holistic view [in investing]. This approach dates from when the new trustee board took office in 2006. We are trying to make sure that a fund manager considers more than just the traditional financial factors. For example, if costs that were external become internal due to regulation, such as carbon limits, the airlines should be valued taking into account carbon limits. It is a question of how the asset manager factors in environmental, governance, and other soft issues in the portfolio." According to this source, taking a more holistic view of a company is a growing trend in the United Kingdom.

Nevertheless, some plans in the United States have been in the forefront of SRI. In 2003, the California Public Employees' Retirement System (CalPERS) announced that it would no longer invest in developing countries that fail to meet its SRI standards, even if the policy takes off an estimated 3 percentage points from the performance of its emerging market portfolios.

Mercer (2009) recently reviewed 16 academic studies about the link between ESG factors and financial performance. Interestingly, the consultant found that 10 of the studies showed a positive relationship between ESG factors and companies' financial performance, 4 showed a neutral relationship, and 2 showed a neutral to negative relationship. Taken together with a 2007 study conducted jointly with the United Nations Environment Programme Finance Initiative (Demystifying Responsible Investment Performance 2007), Mercer found that out of 36 academic studies, 20 showed evidence of a positive relationship between ESG factors and financial performance whereas only 3 demonstrated a fully negative relationship.

7. Challenges

We asked participants, in view of recent market events, what they consider are the major challenges confronting institutional investors, investment consultants, asset managers, and investment banks in the asset management space. Perhaps not surprisingly, sources said the biggest challenge for all is to regain credibility with the investor. Additional challenges specific to each category varied but can be summarized as follows:

- For institutional investors: Pay the pension promise; for small plans, it is also a question of survival.
- For investment consultants: Improve their skill set to be able to deal with more complex investment strategies as well as to add value in asset allocation and risk management.
- For asset managers: Manage with reduced revenues; review the product offering and the business model to respond to changes in future inflows and investor strategies and preferences.
- For investment banks in the asset management space: Put the interests of the investor first.

Challenges Facing Institutional Investors

CIOs at institutional investors cited the need to regain the trust of the board of trustees and plan members after assets tumbled in 2008 and early 2009 as their major challenge. A source at a large European pension fund said, "The whole financial industry lost credibility with the last crisis. As asset managers at a defined-benefit fund, we have to regain credit and the trust of the trustees. This effort will take some time."

Regaining trust will require cooperation from the markets as well as more communication with trustees and plan members about investment risks. A source at a large corporate pension fund said, "To regain credibility, we will have to be transparent and get the trustees to buy in. We will need to communicate more about the risks as well as create a greater understanding of risk. Some notions of risk were observed and communicated, but not the right risks. The dilemma," the source added, "is that if we had set our asset allocation strategy in terms of the risks that we really faced, expected returns would be lower because we would have had to follow a more conservative policy."

The CIO of a defined-benefit (DB) industrywide fund in the Netherlands remarked, "A solid pension has always been taken for granted by the Dutch. Enough has not been done about the risks involved. We are now communicating more on risk."

For persons in defined-contribution (DC) plans, the riskiness of their investments was made all too clear when major indices lost around half of their value in the recent market crash. A source in the United States said, "After recent market losses, DC plans are much less attractive. Individuals have understood that they bear the risk. Investors in DC plans are saying, God help if I retired on 10 March 2009. The money in the bucket would have been pretty low. The employee would be off for retirement with much less money than he or she had counted on. People were burnt with DC plans."

Regaining the confidence of trustees and plan members will also call for better management of expectations. The head of a multiemployer pension fund in Austria commented, "A major challenge institutional investors face is that return expectations are too high in relation to the risk that we can take. Plan member expectations of returns are in the range of 6 percent, but it will be difficult to realize returns of more than 6 percent when government bonds have interest rates of less than 4 percent. You cannot deliver returns that are double those on government bonds."

While sources cited a loss of confidence, they also mentioned the need to resist the temptation to do everything differently. The CIO at a large institutional investor said, "Pension plan members are worried because financial markets have done poorly recently. They have a knee-jerk response; they want to reduce risk. It is our job to counter this knee-jerk response."

The CIO at a large public-sector fund in the United States concurred: "There is the need to resist the urge to try to do everything differently just because one year the strategy did not work. Investing is a continual learning process. Investors must realize that there is risk in investments. The range of outcomes might be very different from what we expect. There is the need for more emphasis on CFA Institute and its work on new investment theories and processes."

One way to avoid a knee-jerk response, sources suggested, is to shift the evaluation of performance to rolling periods of several years. The stakes in delivering the pension promise are potentially high, with some sources questioning if too much has been promised as demographic and macroeconomic trends change.

The head of a public-sector fund in the United Kingdom said, "Schemes will have to change. There are longevity questions and other issues. We might have to go from a final-salary-based pension to a sort of career average and up the retirement age. We will try to improve returns by a more frequent reallocation among asset classes, but in the end, I am afraid the government will have to step in and modify the contract."

The head of a multiemployer pension fund in central Europe remarked, "There are structural changes now happening in the economy. We need to see the large macro developments because they are very important for the fund and society in the future. If we are not able to pay pensions, there will be a lot of social unrest."

For institutional investors that cannot walk away from their obligations, sources said that paying the pension promise in today's highly uncertain low-interest-rate environment is a formidable challenge. A source at a large institutional investor in North America said, "Paying the pension promise is our focus, our greatest concern."

Sources at smaller and/or private-sector funds remarked that survival itself is a challenge. These sources cited losses incurred during the 2008 meltdown, the ability of plan sponsors to continue to finance plans, and the survival of the plan sponsor itself.

A source at a small corporate fund in Belgium said, "What's the biggest challenge? Survival. In the short term, it is very clear that we cannot afford another 2008. Recovery plans have to be implemented, and it will take two to three years before we get comfortable with the funding ratio. By law, a fund has five years to return to a 100 percent funding ratio."

Sources at private-sector pension plans remarked that the survival of the fund depends on the ability to understand the trade-off between the contribution the firm can make and its ability to cover losses in case an investment strategy goes wrong. The managing director of a large private-sector fund in the United Kingdom said, "The real challenge is in articulating what really matters and in understanding if one really can take a risk or if one needs to take the risk off the table. What is the downside, the odds behind a strategy? What is the cash contribution needed from the sponsor if the strategy goes wrong—£150,000 or £2 billion?"

For private-sector funds, the survival of the plan sponsor itself cannot be assumed in today's environment. The CIO at a medium-sized private-sector pension fund remarked, "It's important to understand sponsor-coverage risk. Will the sponsor still be here in 5 or 10 years? There are very few metrics available to help understand sponsor-coverage risk. Is the sponsor able to survive? If not, we will all be looking for new jobs."

To pay the pension promise, sources said that they are adopting different strategies: bringing asset allocation and asset management in-house to gain better control and reduce costs (discussed in Chapters 4 and 5); implementing various immunization or diversification strategies, including enlarging the investable universe and being more active in asset allocation (discussed in Chapter 2); and doing a better job of controlling risk (discussed in Chapter 3). Many large institutional investors on both sides of the Atlantic are using several of these strategies.

The CIO at a large public-sector fund in North America said, "To pay the pensions promise, we have to ensure that costs are down and returns are up. Our strategy is three pronged: to form more alliances to pool assets to have access to investment opportunities, to move more assets to internal active managers, and to invest more in nonpublic investments. We are confident that, as a large fund, we will be able to implement this strategy. But it is different for corporate pension plans because they are exposed to external managers."

Some sources cited the need for more fundamental work on portfolio theory and optimization. The CIO of a public-sector fund in the United States remarked,

> Portfolio theories and traditional portfolio optimization that have been with us since the 1980s are getting stale. There is a need for more work on slicing portfolios by characteristics of assets and how they move in different scenarios. In the past, equities and corporate bonds were considered different asset classes, but in reality, they move together. There is the need to ask how the assets perform during periods of inflation and in strong and weak economies. For example, in the 1980s domestic equities were viewed as one asset class and international equities as another asset class, but they are one global class. Europeans were quicker than Americans to realize this correlation. Then there is the need to look at emerging markets equity and debt and what drives them to perform so well or so poorly. Plus, there is the need for more diversification. Today, it is typical in U.S. pension funds to hold 60–70 percent in equities, and if you hold corporate bond portfolios as well, you are exposed to the same risk factors.

Nevertheless, as hard as plan sponsors try, some sources question the ability of the markets to generate sufficient returns to pay the pension promise given the financial constraints on sponsors. A source at an asset management firm said,

> Funds will not get the returns they need. Return-chasing behavior started after the technology bubble burst in 2000 and we enjoyed low interest rates. With low interest rates, the question became how to get the returns needed. Institutional investors moved into high-return asset classes, but that was the wrong move. It is now clear that we have promised ourselves too much. There are two solutions: go out and look for assets that will produce higher returns—but they are just not there—or look at what we promised and take steps to reduce that—but the political will is not there.

Exhibit 7.1 summarizes the challenges facing institutional investors and strategies for dealing with these challenges.

Challenges Facing Investment Consultants

Sources cited the need to regain the trust of investors as the major challenge for investment consultants as well as for the rest of the industry. Sources agreed that consultants took on the area of most risk in asset allocation but widely faulted consultants for doing a poor job in both asset allocation and manager selection as well as for failing to understand the risk in the investment strategies they use.

Exhibit 7.1. Challenges Facing Institutional Investors and Strategies for Dealing with Them

Challenges	Strategy for Dealing with Challenges
Regain investor confidence	• Communicate with trustees and plan members about investment risk • Manage expectations better
Resist the impulse to do everything differently	• Evaluate performance over rolling periods of several years
For DB plan sponsors: Pay the pension promise in a highly uncertain low-interest rate environment if large and unable to exercise a bankruptcy option Survive if small and able to exercise a bankruptcy option	• If large, bring costs down by moving asset management in-house • Pay more attention to macro, achieve greater diversification, and do more dynamic asset allocation • Align the risk–return appetite and correctly evaluate the ability of the plan sponsor to make a cash contribution if the strategy goes wrong

A source in the Netherlands remarked, "Large consultants in many countries have done a lousy job—lousy in defining the risk budget, in building an efficient portfolio, and in manager selection."

The head of a public-sector pension fund in the United Kingdom bemoaned the fact that consultants failed to understand or communicate the risks inherent in their investment strategies. "Consultants," he said, "could have done a better job highlighting the risks in 2008."

Not all sources faulted consultants, however, for their failure to predict market events. Consultants, after all, were not alone in failing to foresee the market crash. A source at a corporate pension plan in continental Europe observed, "If you look at the advice consultants gave clients a couple of years ago, they were surely off the mark. But then no one saw the crisis coming. Just look at what the experts were saying!"

In addition, some sources remarked that the role of consultants is essentially one of providing comfort to trustees in the form of fiduciary insurance protection. This latter view is widely shared by CIOs at large institutional investors on both sides of the Atlantic.

The CIO of a large public-sector pension fund in the United States that does not use consultants remarked, "Investment consultants are there because of fiduciary insurance protection, but their advice is worth next to nothing. It is a question of the business model: Consultants are there to add comfort. They will never recommend anything different than consensus thinking; it would be treacherous on the downside, and there is no upside."

Sources pointed to new challenges for consultants because the pillars of their approach to asset allocation, diversification, and risk management are not sufficient in today's low-return environment and important structural changes are occurring in the world economy. In particular, sources remarked that a typical consultant's strategy for achieving diversification by hiring multiple managers has not worked.

An industry observer said, "Consultants argue that they diversify the investment risk by giving money to 20–25 managers, but the track record has not been good. Management costs go up, and no one manages the overall process." The problem is that most managers will have approximately the same beta exposures, and therefore, the benefits of diversification are ultimately small.

The CIO at a large institutional investor concurred: "Consultants need to improve their professional skills. They must move away from a business model of advising clients about external managers as a way of making money by running new manager searches every three to four years."

Sources also agreed that the old model of providing value by selecting a benchmark and then selecting managers to outperform the benchmark is of scant interest when the benchmark itself is falling in value. A source at a large U.S. consultancy remarked, "Unless consultants bolster their professional skills, they will be perceived as merely being part of the distribution system of the investment management industry."

Consultants were advised by the sources to bolster their skills in several areas.

First, in asset allocation, they need to improve their skills in a wide range of asset classes. Recent market turmoil has made it painfully clear that returns are driven by asset allocation decisions based on macro views as opposed to managers who are selected according to their perceived ability to pick stocks. Interestingly, in markets dominated by consultants, it has not been unusual to see up to 70 percent of a fund's assets allocated to equity markets.

Over the past decade or more, the investable universe has been extended to new asset classes, thus creating the need for new expertise and for more due diligence. The CIO at a large U.S. corporate pension plan pointed to what he sees as a failure of asset allocation as it is widely practiced today: "Asset allocation is now being done by people in silos, with no view of the trade-offs among the different asset classes. Whoever does asset allocation must be accountable as well as have hands-on experience in running money with different asset classes." As we discussed in Chapters 2 and 5, the extension of the investable universe and the perceived need for a multiplicity of views are opening opportunities for asset managers to play a role in what had been the exclusive domain of consultants.

A source at a large consultancy that has a 10-person hedge fund research team remarked that the big consultancies will have to build up their expertise, especially in alternatives. According to this source,

> In the wake of the Madoff affair and other high-profile investment manager swindles, consultants have come under questioning. We will see a tiering of consultants with small low-cost consultants and larger high-cost consultants. The top-tier consultants will have to build strong research capabilities, especially in the alternatives area. They will have to increase their staff and expertise to include research managers in, for example, hedge funds, private equity, real estate, and commodities.

A multi-asset world is also adding new challenges for consultants in terms of performance measurement and attribution analysis. In a benchmark-relative world, performance measurement is quite straightforward. Did the manager outperform (1) before adjusting for risk, (2) on a risk-adjusted (that is, beta-adjusted) basis, and (3) relative to peers with similar mandates? With an investment goal that cannot be represented by a market benchmark (for example, to earn inflation plus 5 percent) and a multi-asset mandate, the consultant's task is much more complicated. The CIO at a U.K. asset management firm said,

> In a multi-asset world, it is much more difficult to understand if the asset manager is doing a good job. First, because the benchmark is uninvestable, is it possible to outperform with the assets available to the manager? Second, is the return earned commensurate with the opportunities available? Third, how much of the return comes from asset allocation decisions (beta choices) and how much from alpha? Finally, peer comparisons are difficult because the universe is small and mandates tend to be idiosyncratic.

Second, consultants were advised to see asset allocation as a dynamic exercise. With several market crashes in the space of a decade, volatility expected to remain high, and major structural changes underway in the world economy, sources agreed that asset allocation can no longer be seen as a static exercise performed once every few years. Instead, it must become (more) dynamic, perhaps with a tactical element.

The head of a large asset management firm in France said, "In the last few years, the focus has been very micro. It must now become more macro and more long term but not static. The practice of an investment consultant deciding one thing and then setting up core–satellite managers and letting it run without intervening, if not to measure manager performance against the benchmark, has been detrimental to investors. Asset allocation must be dynamic; there must be a tactical element."

Third, as risk management has moved up on the investor's agenda, consultants will need the tools to measure and manage portfolio risk. A source in Germany said, "As consultants, we need to respond on new topics such as risk management. We are now running seminars, talking to customers on risk issues, and discussing new risk management techniques that we are implementing."

Sources mentioned that consultants are not accountable for their investment decisions; some suggested that consultants will have to go beyond just giving advice, eventually teaming up with or selling their organization to those responsible for managing the assets, either an asset management firm or a large institutional investor. This view is quite typical of sources in northern Europe. A source in the Netherlands said, "Consultants will need to take control, fiduciary control, and responsibility. They will have to go one step further than what they now do. We will see a sort of merger with consultants and either large pension funds or asset managers as investors perceive the need to integrate asset allocation and asset management." Indeed, sources remarked that active asset allocation and risk management call for being close to the markets.

Recent market turmoil has posed the question of survival for consultants along with other players in the investment management industry. A fall in the number of assets available for advisement, combined with other (some long-term) trends, is creating a challenging environment for investment consultants. The challenges can be summarized as follows:

• Consulting revenues are down. Two explanations exist for this situation. First, companies are controlling costs by cutting budgets for consultants. Second, some consultants base their fee structure on a percentage of assets they advise on. Similar to asset managers, they have seen income drop as the market value of assets dropped. A consultant in the United States said, "Quite a large portion of our client revenue is asset based. So, the recent market fall is having a negative impact on revenues, which have also become more volatile. This volatility is creating margin pressure given that, at the same time revenues are down, there is the need for more frequent communication with the client and more hand-holding, which is costly. If we had hourly rates, we would see that our remuneration is way down."

• Pension plan sponsors are switching their plans from DB plans to DC plans. This switch is occurring especially in countries in which consultants are strongest. For example, in the United Kingdom a recent survey by the Association of Consulting Actuaries (2009) found that among the 309 participating funds with total assets of more than £138 billion, 87 percent were now closed to new entrants; of these, 18 percent were also closed to all future accruals for existing participants. Although some sources pointed out that assets in DB funds are expected to grow before they start to shrink, new business opportunities will be harder to find. Already, by year-end 2008, assets in DC plans were estimated to represent 45 percent of the total assets in pension funds, up from 30 percent 10 years ago (Towers Watson 2009). Sources remarked that not much work is available for consultants with DC plans—only a tiny portion of the work involved with a DB plan. As one consultant put it, "We will not make much money on these." In addition, as mentioned in Chapter 5, asset managers with all-weather investment products are playing an increasingly important role in the DC arena.

- Many large institutional investors are bringing asset allocation (and in some cases, asset management) in-house, thereby reducing or cutting out the consultant altogether, except maybe for an asset/liability management study every 10–15 years. In addition, some of the largest pension funds in northern Europe are now competing with consultants for the business of smaller funds, as discussed in Chapter 5.

- Many of the consultants' clients are small pension funds whose survival is not guaranteed. A source at a large institutional investor in North America that does not use consultants said, "Investment consultants— indeed, the whole investment management industry—must try to be relevant to small corporate funds that have a survival issue. If you work with entities that have a survival issue, how can you get fees out of that?"

Consulting firms are dealing with the challenges in several ways:

- First, consultants are trying to increase revenues and add value. A source in the United Kingdom said, "The old-fashioned model was time and materials—that is, an hourly fee. Now, we charge a management fee of a few basis points on the assets we consult on. We are also evolving our business model, going in the direction of the Dutch consultancy Cardano, which does everything except manage the assets directly: asset/liability management, asset allocation, tactical asset allocation, and manager selection. The idea is to add more intellectual capital and more asset management. Clients no longer want to pay for information; information costs nothing today, so we need to get paid on intellectual capital. The U.K. market is moving more toward delegated fund management, and we, as a consultant, are evolving our business model to offer all solutions."

- Second, consulting firms are controlling costs. Even among those that are not reducing their headcount, many have imposed hiring and compensation freezes. In mid-2009, a source in the United States said, "We have been in business for 35 years and never laid anyone off. We do not want to change that now, but we have a hiring freeze in place. There are some exceptions, but we are being very careful. There is also a freeze on compensation and profit sharing, which will be on the down side this year."

- Third, consulting firms are exploring opportunities to merge or sell their businesses. A consultant in Germany said, "Some consolidation is going on in the sector. We are being approached by other consultancies to explore possibilities to merge." A source at a large institutional investor in North America observed, "We are already seeing consolidation among the consultants." Indeed, in June of 2009, two of the biggest players—Towers Perrin and Watson Wyatt—announced a deal in which the two organizations would merge, creating a firm with expected annual revenues of US$3 billion. **Exhibit 7.2** summarizes the challenges facing investment consultants and strategies for dealing with them.

Exhibit 7.2. Challenges Facing Investment Consultants and Strategies for Dealing with Them

Challenges	Strategy(ies) for Dealing with Challenges
Regain investor confidence	Communicate more and do more hand-holding
Add value as investment strategies pursued by institutional investors become more complex	• Bolster competencies in risk budgeting, asset allocation, and new/multi-asset classes • Attract, maintain, and develop talent to accomplish the above
Maintain organization in face of lower and/or more volatile revenues in the crisis/post-crisis period	• Change the basis on which fees are charged • Reduce headcount and/or compensation
Survive as funds switch from DB to DC and large investors increasingly bring asset allocation in-house	• Enlarge the service offering to include, for example, fiduciary management • Merge or form alliances with asset managers or institutional investors

Challenges Facing Asset Managers

"The major challenge for asset managers," one industry source said, "is credibility and the need to regain investor confidence. Even though asset managers were not at the center of recent turmoil, did not take extravagant bonuses, and on the whole, did not lose investor money as the financial system blew up, there has been a tremendous spillover effect." Sources agreed.

Among sources at institutional investors, asset managers are largely perceived as putting their own interests before those of the client. The CIO at a large U.S. corporate pension plan remarked, "Asset managers have to deliver what they are supposed to deliver, but they are not delivering excess returns for their clients. Their concern is to gather assets to make money for the firm, not for the clients."

Institutional investors suggested that one way the trust might be reestablished is for asset managers to align their interests with those of the investor. Institutional investors remarked that asset managers are closer to the markets than the consultant and should play a bigger role in advising on their mandates, even when this might go against the short-term interests of the manager (some considered this wishful thinking).

The head of a public-sector pension fund in the United Kingdom said,

> We would like the asset manager to pick up his head and look at the world. The asset manager knows even better than the consultant what asset classes we should be in and out of. If the manager is a multi-asset manager, he gets the feedback from the market. If the relationship is to be a long one, he should also advise the investor as to which asset class he should be in or out of. The asset manager should work together with the consultant. As it is now, we give a benchmark to a manager; the manager is able to understand if the benchmark is not so efficient. If the manager sees that some parts are not so efficient, he should advise the client, but he does not. The manager has a business risk that is against the interests of the investor.

The head of a corporate pension plan in Austria concurred:

> We would appreciate it if a fund manager got involved to a certain degree in asset allocation; tell the investor that the fund will not return in the future and say "Let's discuss." If the manager is managing a long portfolio, I would expect the manager to have a view on the short side and to say, if necessary, "This is not really the right asset class to be in at the moment." Only a few managers are willing to do that. It might be against the short-term interest of the manager, but I believe it is in his or her long-term interest.

Sources in wealth management also identified the need to regain investor trust as the biggest challenge in the aftermath of 2008. A source at a private bank in Luxembourg said, "Clients are moving away from banks not so much because of fees but because they believe that the bank is not secure—the bank has lost their trust. In the past, it was a question of trust between the client and the adviser, but the investor now looks at the institution, the time deposits, if the bank is investing the assets of the client, the legal structure, and investor protection."

Similar to the retail investor, a high-net-worth individual's trust in the asset manager is largely related to his or her trust in the markets. When the markets tumbled, trust in the investment management industry also tumbled. As one source put it, "Bubbles come and bubbles go and leave a lot of people angry. Asset managers need a trust proposition."

Although the Anglo-Saxon investment culture accepts a great deal of risk in the pursuit of higher returns, continental European investors are more concerned about the safety of their savings. Indeed, sources remarked that investors' return expectations are several percentage points lower in continental Europe than in the United Kingdom. During recent movements that caused financial markets to fall sharply in 2008 and then climb back up in 2009, investors in continental Europe remained largely on the sidelines.

An industry observer in Germany said,

> The year 2008 was not the first time that markets have gone through such a phase in my short time in the industry. Losses this time around are even greater than losses incurred when the technology, media, and telecommunications bubble burst in 2000. The recent fall will have a very strong impact on the industry. A large number of investors have lost confidence in the worth of long-term investments in stocks. Fund investment is now perceived as being very risky, very dangerous. The belief in fund management as a solution for pension savings has been hampered.

This source observed that since the crash and despite the strong performance of equities as of the second quarter of 2009, mutual fund sales to German retail investors were close to zero for the year 2009. "The problem," according to this source, "is to win back investor confidence. Strong market movements since the spring of 2009, with markets up sharply without any fundamental reason for their being up, is reinforcing people's perception that the markets are a casino. It has not helped win trust for the markets. Now the fear is even greater."

Because the sale of investment products still goes largely through independent financial advisers in such countries as the United States and the United Kingdom and through banks in continental Europe, asset managers will also have to regain the trust of the distribution network.

A source in Austria, where the investment culture is very similar to that of Germany, said, "Asset managers need to regain the trust of the investor and of the sales force in the distribution network as well as in the banks. They are bearing the bulk of investors' complaints. If the markets do not perform in the next one to two years, it will be a very big problem for the industry. We will not be able to say that 2008 was an aberration."

Regaining the confidence of investors will also call for a better management of expectations. The question one might ask is, what is the promise? Sources agreed that the asset manager industry as a whole cannot generate above-market returns.

One source stressed the need to not overpromise:

The biggest challenge is to align expectations and delivery, to produce results consistent with expectations. Unrealistic expectations end in disappointment. In long only, the biggest return the industry delivers is the market return. Active managers return only a small portion of the total return. Is it positive net of fees? There are people who go into a casino. Anyone going into a casino knows full well that the casino does not expect to lose money; an embedded portion of the returns goes to the house. But the client also expects that there is a wide dispersion of what can occur. And then there is the entertainment factor. Active managers have tons of stories to tell—they are good at cocktail talk. They sound as if they know more; and then there is the possibility that they can do well, and in many cases, they do indeed do well.

A source in Germany called for better communication with the investor about risk and opportunities, especially in regards to stock funds:

To say "I am an asset manager for class X of stocks, and I will beat the market" is not true. But it is true that some asset managers are more successful than others. Quality counts along with good research and good management, which can help one asset manager beat the market more often than others. But at the end of the day, it is clear that the average manager will not beat the market. There is the need to redefine the offer in active management. The asset manager has not provided protection. He cannot say to the investor that he did a good job if markets were down 40 percent and the fund was down only 38 percent.

This source reflected the thinking of some asset managers who define their role as one of asset allocation, risk management, and liquidity management. A source in France said, "What can the asset manager really manage? Risk, but not market returns. Asset managers have been too focused on returns, on alpha, but this return is something they cannot deliver. But asset managers can help determine what is a good risk for any single investor. Better risk management is an enormous added value in asset management."

A Challenging Environment for Asset Managers

In addition to creating a problem of credibility for asset managers, the crash of 2008 has, one source said, "turned the industry upside down." The fall in assets under management has combined with other (some long-term) trends to create a very challenging environment. Although many of these trends were already in progress before the crash, sources agreed that the trends were both amplified and accelerated by the crash. The trends are summarized as follows:

• With revenues down, many asset management firms are struggling to survive at a time when servicing the client requires a greater ability than before to analyze the environment not only to generate returns but also to manage risk. A source at a corporate pension fund remarked,

> What is the function of the asset manager? Ultimately, it is to get income from serving the client, so client needs should be central. To give sound advice, asset managers need to analyze the environment, so they need to have analysts, including macroeconomists, on board. There is the need for more in-house buy-side research. But most asset managers are not able to make the requisite investment; they are struggling to survive. I believe that 30–50 percent will disappear. From the macro point of view, there is no place for them anymore.

• Faith in the ability of asset managers to *consistently* add value has been shaken. Many investors have concluded that active management actually destroys value. To the extent that investors can accept market returns, many are putting more assets under passive management. Institutional investors as well as high-net-worth and retail investors are also making this move, leading to a proliferation of cheap beta products. The move toward cheap beta products is further depressing revenues for firms already hit by a fall in assets under management. Faith in the ability of alternatives to deliver has also been shaken. Hedge funds marketed themselves as absolute-return funds but lost money during the crash. An industry observer commented, "Hedge funds overpromised and underdelivered. You cannot suddenly switch your bark and say 'We outperformed our peers.' It is the mismanagement of a promise."

• New sources of business are becoming increasingly difficult to find and capture. As one source put it, "Asset managers are all swimming in the same pool, fighting over fewer dollars to manage."

Several reasons are contributing to this decline in new sources. First, pension assets, a key pillar of growth for the industry since the 1970s, will become a dwindling source of new business as DB pension plans are closed, DC plan members seek greater security for their investments, and large institutional investors (increasingly) bring asset management in-house. The CIO at a large northern European fund shared his vision for the future of the industry: "As the large long-term players increasingly manage their assets in-house, the traditional asset manager will retain only the retail business, small wholesale business, and maybe insurance."

Second, retail investors, especially in continental Europe, are hesitant to get back into the markets after suffering losses several times in one decade. A source in Germany said, "In a normal year, we would see €30 billion in net flows into mutual funds, but we have not had a normal year in a long time. Investors see the game as too risky. In 2009, sales were flat; 2008 saw net outflows of €29 billion; and the year before, the outflows were €20 billion to €30 billion."

Third, wealth is being transferred from developed countries to developing countries. A source at a private bank in Geneva remarked, "Asset growth in developed markets will be limited in the short to medium term. Everyone knows that there is a shift of wealth from West to East."

Sources expect that this new wealth—either institutional or private—will stay in the developing world where there are more opportunities. The vice chairman of a large international firm said,

> The pension fund industry is developing in emerging markets in Asia and Latin America where the savings rates are high, but the focus is on national or regional products. People in these countries are now moving out of savings accounts held in banks and into mutual funds in the form of indexed funds and exchange-traded funds [ETFs]. But the money is going to stay in emerging markets—maybe not domestic, but regional. For example, Chilean pension funds will stay invested in Latin America or diversify into other emerging regions; Chinese money will stay in China or diversify into the region.

Sources also noted that this new wealth has different demands. A private banker in Geneva remarked,

> The new high-net-worth individuals in emerging markets are reinvesting their wealth in entrepreneurial activities or investing in local industry, not in pure asset management products. In the past, investors had assets that they were leveraging and, with margin calls, had to pledge additional money. The new wealthy are not coming to the bank with US$10 million and asking us to manage it. Rather, they will say, "Here is US$2 million to invest in the markets. I have a house in Ibiza, an old car collection, and so on. How much will you lend me on this?" Then they go off and develop their own industrial ventures and investment ideas. These clients now have more information than the banks. Private banks will need to offer different types of services, such as loans and networking capability. It will be difficult for asset management firms in the West to capture these assets.

How Asset Managers Are Dealing with a Challenging Environment

Asset management firms are dealing with the challenges in several ways.

First, the industry is restructuring. Sources remarked that the whole financial services industry is probably oversized relative to the real economy.

Some of the restructuring is purely defensive—an attempt to improve the profitability of firms hit by a fall in assets under management as the markets crashed and as investors moved their assets to such lower-cost products as bonds, index funds, and ETFs. Some firms are responding by reducing headcounts in an effort to realize gains in efficiency. Sources estimated that employment in the industry is down about 30 percent compared with the highs in 2007. Others firms are being more proactive by trying to gather assets to exploit economies of scale. A source at a large international firm said,

> Traditional asset management is nearing its demise. This decline has been happening for several years, but it has been accelerated by recent market events. If you look at the list of traditional long-only managers five years ago, many have now merged or moved into alternatives. For example, Merrill Lynch, which had acquired Mercury Asset Management [1997], then merged with BlackRock [2006], which then acquired Barclays Global Investors [2009]. The recent Black-Rock acquisition of Barclays Global Investors and iShares has other large players looking for ways to exploit economies of scale, which is one driver of merger and acquisition activity now going on in the sector.

Some players are getting out of the market altogether. One observer of the European industry said, "There is a clear trend toward a lot of asset management firms being for sale as large financial services groups divest various business units to reshape their balance sheets. We will see a lot of mergers." Another source in Europe said,

> Over the next two to three years, we will see a big push for consolidation; the number of firms will probably shrink significantly. But this will require the willingness to buy and the willingness to sell. Second-tier banking and insurance firms that got into asset management will realize that they cannot attract the best talent or pay for it. Over the past three years, they have seen that in-house asset managers cannot generate significant returns. These organizations will sell the production function in exchange for access to distribution.

Other sources remarked that the industry is being restructured by investors as they withdraw their money from managers that have not been able to produce alpha. A source in Germany commented, "Those who call themselves active but only replicate the index have had their time; the market has decided that they are too expensive."

In private wealth management, the additional problem exists that is posed by regulation and attempts to control tax evasion. Similar to asset managers, private banks are responding by reducing costs. A source in Switzerland said,

> My subjective view is that, as fees are down about 30 percent based on assets under management, the private wealth industry—in terms of the number of products, sales teams, and asset managers—will have to shrink by a similar number. We have already seen the industry shrink by 10–15 percent, and there is another 10–15 percent to go. A high correlation exists between the level of stock markets and the profitability of private banks. Even with the markets up in 2009, they are still lower than two years ago. Many people are being laid off. Other short-term measures to reduce costs are being adopted, such as putting pressure on suppliers or reducing working hours.

As is happening with asset management units, some financial groups are divesting (parts of) their private banking units. A source at a private bank in Luxembourg remarked, "Many players are withdrawing from some markets and putting private banking units up for sale. For example, many private banks are withdrawing from international markets to concentrate their efforts in their home markets or trying to raise cash by selling noncore businesses, such as ING Group looking to sell its Asian unit or many German banks who have sold off their private bank entities."

As for private banks divesting their asset management units, a source at a private bank in Switzerland said, "Those who can afford it are adapting a wait-and-see attitude. Others will break down and sell. The industry will shrink by up to 30 percent. Julius Baer Group, for example, is splitting asset management and private banking, with the objective of selling the pieces. We get two or three offers a month from firms wanting to sell their asset management units. When we tell them what we are willing to pay, they refuse to sell."

Second, asset management firms are reviewing their product offering. In the very near term, sources expect that the underfunding of pension plans will drive inflows as plan sponsors have to top up; in the not-so-distant future, sources expect that inflows will come from Baby Boomers as they retire with their lump-sum pension payments or from defined-contribution and individual savings plans. Asset managers are adapting their offerings in several ways.

First, concerning institutional investors, asset managers are responding by building up their capability in asset allocation and enlarging the universe of asset classes under management, including alternatives. One source commented, "Most traditional asset managers have merged or gone into alternatives. Gartmore Investment has turned itself into a hedge fund. Schroder Investment Management has moved into absolute returns. J.P. Morgan does just about everything—or at least it tries to. As for ourselves, we have index funds and ETFs, emerging markets, alternatives, and multi-asset-class portfolios that do asset allocation."

Nevertheless, the ability of asset managers to extend the product range is limited—either by law or by investment culture—in some countries. A source in Germany remarked, "Investment funds offered by asset managers must, by law, be based on listed securities. Private equity and alternatives are not in funds that are based on the UCITS directive."[27] Although it would be possible for funds designed especially for institutional investors, such as pension funds or insurance companies (the German Spezialfonds), to be in alternatives, the source added that very little use of alternatives by institutional investors occurs in Germany (they are perceived to be too risky). Rather, 85–90 percent of institutional assets are in bonds because, according to law or on demand of the institutional investor, funds must produce a stable 3–4 percent return every year.

As asset managers move from offering products to offering solutions, they are becoming more knowledgeable about the risks and working to improve their risk management systems. One source remarked, "In providing solutions, asset managers will need to think about risk–return scenarios and make clients risk aware because the ability to take risk is the only real asset the investor has. Asset managers will need to measure risk, understand how to put risk effectively into the fund, and eventually work together with the consultant in the risk-budgeting exercise."

The ability of asset managers to better manage risk and offer some degree of downside protection is also important to individual investors. Referring to the fact that mutual funds failed to protect investors as markets crashed in 2008, a source in Germany said, "There is the need to redefine the offer in active management in the direction of offering asset allocation, to move away from the idea of dedicated funds invested in only one segment to funds that change with the market situation. This redefining will require a mechanism to change the asset allocation when the market loses a given percentage of its value."

The need to shift the offering from investment products for accumulating wealth to products that offer yield and protection against various risks has been identified as a major trend in the United States, where an estimated 77 million Baby Boomers will be retiring shortly. Using data from the U.S. Census Bureau and a 2004 survey of consumer finances, McKinsey & Company (2006) forecasted that by 2010 almost two-thirds of all investable assets held by U.S. investors would be controlled by retirees or near-retirees. According to McKinsey, its affluent consumer survey showed that the retirement wave is fueling demand for investment products that mitigate various risks (see **Figure 7.1**).

More generally, as the world moves from DB to DC plans, sources mentioned that the financial services industry will have to meet two big challenges: to engineer products that offer some sort of downside protection and to reduce the overall cost

[27]The UCITS directive is the Undertakings for Collective Investments in Transferable Securities directive.

Figure 7.1. **Percentage of Respondents Answering the Question: "How Interested Would You Be in Purchasing Financial Products That Would Protect You Against Each of the Following Risks?"**

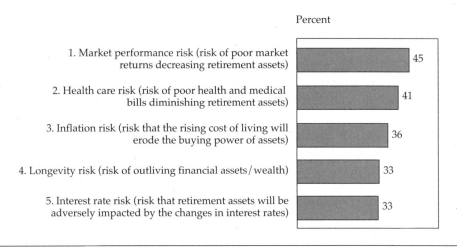

Source: Based on data from McKinsey & Company (2006).

to the beneficiary. A U.K. asset manager said, "In moving from DB to DC plans, there is a shift of interest. The objectives are determined by the beneficiary as opposed to the plan sponsor. This shift will require asset managers to dedicate time, resources, and money to learn the real value of investment to the individual." Another source commented on the need to reduce management costs. According to this source, "To service DC plan members, the industry needs to become more efficient." Sources believe that it will take awhile before it is clear what the shift from DB to DC plans means for the asset management industry. But one source predicted, "Within a 10-year time frame, growth will be driven by life insurance products and annuities in the DC market and by mutual funds outside of the DC market."

Sources also expect to see a consolidation in the number of funds available, at least in Europe. According to one source, "Firms must work to improve product development and the product range. There are now far too many products in the European mutual fund industry. The minimum size to run a fund is US$200 million to US$250 million. Below this, it is not financially viable. But a lot of funds operate in Europe with US$20 million to US$30 million under management. With so little under management, the manager is not motivated to do a good job for the client." Another source concurred and added, "The situation is unsustainable." According to figures from the European Fund and Asset Management Association (EFAMA 2009), as of mid-year 2009 there were 52,748 funds in Europe managing a total of €6.4 trillion. The average European fund manages around €120 million. For comparison, as of year-end 2008, there were 8,022 U.S. registered mutual funds managing a total of US$9.6 trillion (Investment Company Institute 2009, Table 1). The average U.S. fund manages US$1.2 billion or almost seven times that of the average European fund.

Third, asset management firms are reviewing their business model. Sources are almost unanimous in their perception that the industry is becoming polarized with, on the one hand, a small number of very big firms with an all-encompassing set of product offerings plus a service model and, on the other hand, a large number of small specialist boutiques. In this scenario, midsized firms would be squeezed out because they would not be able to realize economies of scale and would not have the resources to build either strong research teams, the platforms needed to serve the institutional investor, or a distribution network.

Sources believe the days of the traditional asset manager are numbered. A consultant in the United States commented, "The traditional manager is squeezed between passive managers and hedge funds. People no longer want a (traditional) product with a 2 percent management fee." As already mentioned in Chapter 4, the ability of the large indexers to bring management costs down to several basis points has allowed them to hang on to business with large institutional investors as the latter bring asset management in-house. As mentioned in that chapter, institutional investors realize that they cannot achieve meaningful savings bringing U.S. index funds in-house, whereas they believe that they can reduce the cost of active management by a factor of 10.

A source from Germany summed up the consensus perception:

> As passive investing grows, players in the market will need to become big enough to do passive. They will face the same problem as depository banks in Germany. There were many banks, but now there are very few as low margins created the need for high volume. In passive management, managers work for a fee of 10 bps—maybe the big ones work for even less—versus 40–50 bps for an active manager. There is not room for many players. Investors are taking a closer look at fees. It will not be easy to get the fees of the past few years. If a manager takes 2 percent, investors do not want that kind of investment. Asset managers will have to be either a big passive player or a niche player that can consistently produce alpha.

Niche players might, nevertheless, be vulnerable. One source remarked, "The rise of specialists will have business risks when the asset class is out of favor. Also, the niche cannot be too small or too trendy to bet the whole business on one asset class. Specializing in real estate might be all right, but not specializing in forestry."

A few sources disagreed with the prevailing view that the industry is moving toward a polarized condition that will see the disappearance of medium-sized managers. One of these said, "It is not size that matters but the culture of asset management. Some midsized firms focus on asset management, and they are continuing to win business. The model works very well if there is respect between the front and back offices, no stars, and high staff retention. Some very large asset managers almost blew up or lost money in 2008. Why do people look at assets under management and not the profitability of the asset manager?"

As for private banks, they are also reviewing their business model as their clients still feel stung with recent losses and high management costs. In an attempt to keep the client, many banks are now offering such cheaper products as ETFs and getting their revenues from advice as they try to manage clients more efficiently. An industry observer in Switzerland remarked, "Big institutions are trying to service customers, especially those with US$500,000 to US$2 million, more efficiently. They are structuring the mass affluent business more like retail but giving it the look and feel of private wealth management—some perks, but overall, the cost basis will go down for the bank. They will bring costs down by offering standardized portfolios with ETFs or passive products; the bank will keep the margin."

Under pressure from governments wanting to control tax evasion and from investors asking for greater transparency, sources reported that private banks are also moving toward an onshore model. One source commented,

> We will see an end to offshore as it used to be—that is, a way to make revenues disappear from the tax collector. There is a very strong push among OECD [Organisation for Economic Co-Operation and Development] nations to end tax evasion. Tax treaties are now being renegotiated. Within 10 years, offshore banking will disappear from most financial centers, although some might remain in the Caribbean Islands. So, countries like Switzerland, Luxembourg, and the Channel Islands will need to have another unique selling proposition. A strong currency, a stable political system, and bankers with talent will not be enough. What else? Lower costs? Better performance?

In reviewing their business model, players in the financial services sector are also questioning where they want to be in regards to the manufacturing and distribution of investment products. Sources agreed that the trend now is away from open architecture and toward guided architecture. A source in the United Kingdom remarked, "The industry is going from open architecture to guided architecture, in which firms offer mostly in-house products but a limited list of third-party products. In the past, firms dealt with every fund manager that came in and said, 'Put my products in your offering.' Going forward, they will be making a selection of 10–15 houses maximum that can deliver product depth."

For managers that are used to marketing their products to the CIOs of DB plans, the demise of these plans poses the problem of how to capture future flows as plan members make their own investment decisions. A source at a major player said, "In the past, you just needed to know 100 pension funds around the world and deal on a wholesale basis. But going forward, most institutional investors' assets will be in bonds; savings will be more at the retail level. The issue for asset managers is how to gain access to saved assets. Asset managers are becoming wholesalers to distribution."

In continental Europe, most retail investment products are sold through the banks; in the United Kingdom and United States, the independent financial adviser plays a major role. A source in the United Kingdom said, "Wholesale will remain, but the role once played by pension funds will be played by financial institutions, such as universal banks. The financial institution becomes the client; the asset manager will do product design to the client's specifications."

This role change raises two issues: first, gaining access to distribution and second, negotiating the revenue split. Sources remarked that it will be difficult (although not impossible) for small- and medium-sized asset managers to gain access to distribution. They will have difficulty building distribution skills and brand awareness and will need to have products that consistently perform well. A source in Germany said,

> Of the German retail investors, 70 percent buy their investment products through the banks, although some use multiple channels. It is possible to get into retail distribution but only if you have a really good product. Some very large asset managers have stumbled with performance and cannot get distribution, but take Carmignac Gestion. It has a very good product and has managed to go from €0 to €10 billion in the German retail market via independent financial advisers, internet sales, and also banks. If an asset manager has a very good product, German banks are not closed.

In regards to the revenue split, negotiation will be a question of the relative strength of the distributor and the producer. In the Italian market, distribution typically takes 90 percent of the revenues (this split has been identified as one cause of the relative weakness of the Italian asset management industry). In Spain, distribution's share of revenues is typically around 70–85 percent; in France, where the asset management industry is relatively strong, distribution's share is around 60 percent. A source at a large asset management firm sees the asset manager being pushed back to become a provider of content. According to this source, "There is a lot of intermediation in a DC retail market. But if the distributor gives only 10–15 percent to the factory, it cannot expect that much for 10 percent. The manufacturer will be able to train the distributor's teams but will not be able to accompany the distributor to sell the product locally."

A final consideration on distribution is what percentage of products will be sold over the internet and the implications for branding. Sources in some countries mentioned that sophisticated people are purchasing investment products, such as index funds and ETFs, over the internet. One source said,

> Take a product like iShares. It is a retail product. The advantage of iShares for the retail investor is that it is cheap; the disadvantage is that it does not pay commissions, so it is not so attractive for distribution. The question is, What percentage of sales of similar products will be e-commerce? Branding will be important in e-commerce. In the DC market, the question is, What marketing

choice to make, branded or unbranded? Do you do branded products that are more expensive, or do you have an institutional unbranded product and also do white label for third parties, such as retail banks and insurance companies? It is hard to say which way the market will go—branded products or white label products.

Exhibit 7.3 summarizes the challenges facing asset managers and strategies for dealing with them.

Exhibit 7.3. Challenges Facing Asset/Wealth Managers and Strategies for Dealing with Them

Challenges	Strategies for Dealing with Challenges
Regain investor confidence	• Better manage expectations and align the promise with the ability to deliver (relative to retail investors and distribution, hope that markets stabilize along with fundamentals) • Play a bigger role in asset allocation, even if it means going against short-term business interests • Redefine the promise in active management as one of asset allocation and risk/liquidity management
Manage with reduced revenues as a result of both short- and long-term factors (DB plans being phased out and DC plans bringing in lower assets, higher costs per employee; large institutional investors bringing asset management in-house; new sources of wealth are in developing countries and expected to stay there)	• Reduce headcount and/or compensation • Seek greater economies of scale through merger and acquisition • Leave the market altogether
Review the product/service offering as institutional investors shift the assets to absolute returns, DC assets overtake DB assets, retiring Baby Boomers change investment objectives, and new wealth wants different services	• Build asset allocation and risk management/ budgeting capability • Expand asset classes under management, including alternatives • Provide all-weather asset allocation products for the individual investor • Bring down costs for DC products • Respond to product/service needs of new high-net-worth individuals in emerging countries
Review the business model as the environment changes and the industry moves toward a polarization between very large firms and small specialist firms	• Achieve economies of scale and/or select specialist niche(s) • Move from open to guided architecture • Separate production and distribution; with other financial institutions replacing CIOs at pension funds as buyers of investment products, secure an adequate deal in revenue sharing • For private banks, switch to advice-based revenues and offer more efficient products; manage the mass affluent more efficiently; move to an onshore model

Challenges Facing Investment Banks in the Asset Management Space

Although investment banks will likely play a bigger role in asset management, at least with products for corporate defined-benefit plan sponsors, most sources believe that their presence in the asset management space has been hampered by recent market events. Their brands have been damaged, and problems with their capital base will at least temporarily limit their ability to participate in the pensions buyout market. Nevertheless, as the authors were writing this monograph in early 2010, UBS announced that it was creating a new insurance and pensions industry group. The press qualified the move as a clear sign that investment banks were returning to a business from which many had pulled back during the crisis.

Other challenges for investment banks in the asset management space include the poor performance of derivatives and other structured products during the crisis (although there is disagreement here) and a transactional view of the relationship with the investor.

In addition, as already mentioned in Chapter 5, large institutional investors are increasingly pooling assets to capture investment opportunities, thereby cutting out investment banks. Some are also engineering their own liability-driven investment (LDI) strategies without the investment banks. A source at a large institutional investor in North America said, "We don't work with investment banks for LDI but do this ourselves, investing in assets that perform similar to our liabilities, without the use of, for example, interest rate swaps."

Even sources that are working with investment banks for treasury-like products said that in the post–Lehman Brothers period, they are being cautious. A source at a large northern European corporate pension fund said, "We deal with investment banks for treasury products; they are the main providers of derivatives and swaps. But now there are fewer investment banks around. I think that we will see a stricter risk policy with respect to investment banks, limiting the allocation for business with a specific bank to achieve more diversification."

Exhibit 7.4 summarizes the challenges facing investment banks in the asset management business.

Exhibit 7.4. Challenges Facing Investment Banks in the Asset Management Business

Challenges

- Brands damaged, capital base eroded by recent market events
- Derivatives did not deliver during the crisis (mixed views)
- Transactional view of relationship with investors
- Large institutional investors pooling assets for investment opportunities, cutting out investment banks
- Institutional investors are more cautious on counterparty risk exposure, seeking more diversification

8. Employment and Compensation Trends

The recent market turmoil has affected the investment management industry in terms of employment and compensation trends. Although the situation is clearly in a flux as markets recover (sources said the year 2009 was literally split in two), some effects will be more long lasting. To reveal the trends, we talked to six executive recruiters and asked institutional investors, investment consultants, and asset managers where, given recent events, they thought future opportunities existed in terms of professional profiles and asset classes. We will start by looking at overall employment and compensation trends as they emerged in the third quarter of 2009, and then we will look at the details of where sources believe future opportunities exist.

Trends in Recruitment

Sources at executive recruitment firms in North America and Europe reported that they had between 20 and 55 percent fewer search mandates in the asset and wealth management industry in 2009 compared with 2008. The drop in overall searches was attributed to downsizing at large asset management firms as the latter tried to maintain profitability with assets under management (AUM) falling and investors preferring lower-margin products. Sources at recruitment firms, however, cautioned that they have only a partial view of the employment picture. Following the market crash, many asset management firms reduced their headcounts by as much as 25 percent and filled middle management positions internally by moving people around within the firm. It should also be noted that, as sources at recruitment firms remarked, much of the hiring that happened in 2009 was through direct contacts or other channels.

Speaking in the third quarter of 2009, a source at a recruitment firm in Germany said, "Our expectation is that the number of searches this year will be down 50 percent over last year. This decline is the result of decreased revenues at asset management firms. The larger asset managers especially have reduced headcounts in sales, marketing, portfolio management, and back office. Our only mandates this year have been for senior management roles and sometimes specialist functions."

Godliman Partners, a recruitment firm that has been tracking gross hiring figures in the industry in the United Kingdom for the last seven years, estimated that, given the volume of work in progress as of September 2009, overall hiring in asset management would be down around 50 percent in 2009 compared with 2008. Specifically, they compared the first nine months of 2009 with the same period in

2008 and found that hiring was down 54 percent in equities, 51 percent in fixed income, and 61 percent in institutional distribution. This decline followed previous year declines in recruiting of 39 percent in equities, 44 percent in fixed income, and 24 percent in institutional distribution (that is, for 2008 compared with 2007). Most of the decrease in hiring for institutional distribution occurred in the last quarter of 2008, after the collapse of Lehman Brothers. On the upside, as of the beginning of 2009, Godliman found that there was a pronounced trend of hiring by new market entrants, namely hedge funds, foreign (mainly U.S.) firms expanding into Europe, and private equity firms—all trying to develop the institutional asset management sales channel in the Europe, Middle East, and Africa (EMEA) region.

A recruiter in the United States observed in late 2009,

> Overall job searches for the asset and wealth management industry were down 25–30 percent during the first three quarters of 2009 compared with the same period in 2008. Even though markets are now up, profitability is not following. After the market crash, investors switched to lower-margin products, such as fixed income, or they are getting equity exposure in a cheaper way, such as through exchange-traded funds [ETFs] or collective investment trusts [CITs], although we have not seen a lot of recruitment in these areas.

Nevertheless, sources remarked that recruiting has picked up since the second half of 2009. A source at a recruitment firm in the United Kingdom said, "The year 2009 can be divided in two. The first half was very slow after the free fall of the markets that occurred at the end of 2008 and the first quarter of 2009. Firms were focused on survival. As of midyear, with the markets up, firms realized that they needed to begin to plan. We began to see a pickup in hiring, and it is now a definite trend."

Trends in Compensation

We also asked sources at recruitment firms in North America and Europe about trends in compensation. According to sources, salaries for new recruits were flat for 2009 compared with 2008, although reduced or deferred bonuses were pushing overall compensation down.

A source in Germany remarked, "The base salary has not changed substantially compared with 2008. Professionals often moved on at the same level regarding their base salary. But bonus guarantees were rather rare. Bonus payouts were reduced by up to 50–75 percent, which brought overall compensation down 25–30 percent."

According to Godliman Partners,

> While base salaries in 2009 did not vary greatly from 2008 levels, bonus levels for fiscal year 2008 paid in 2009 were down between 20–40 percent across the board. We would expect fiscal year 2009 bonus levels—to be paid in 2010—to be down by as much as 40 percent compared with 2008 bonuses. The reason for this is that most firms started the year with around 40 percent less assets under management, hence a 40 percent reduction in fees. Over the year, many firms have recouped much of that loss. But overall P&Ls [profit and loss statements] were much weaker than in 2008, when they only suffered asset loss in the last quarter.

A source at a recruitment firm in the United States remarked that, although base salaries at asset and wealth management firms were moving up modestly—about 3 percent in 2009 compared with 2008—it might be a matter of the math—that is, salaries are calculated by adding together the total salaries and dividing by the number of employees. According to the Russell Reynolds Associates 2009 report, "Defining the New Reality for the Asset and Wealth Management Industry: Recruiting and Compensation Trends," 2009 bonus pools will vary considerably according to the firm's investment performance, asset retention, and how quickly and deeply the firm trimmed its cost structure when the downturn hit. The report concludes that for firms that weathered the crisis better, 2009 bonuses will be down by single-digit percentages whereas for others, the bonus pools are likely to be down 20–35 percent from 2008.

Similar figures were cited by McKinsey, which estimated in its *Asset Management Survey 2009* (2009a) that for asset management firms in Western Europe, the 2009 profit pool would be down 25 percent compared with 2008 and down 55 percent compared with 2007 (see **Figure 8.1**). Estimates for U.S. asset management firms were similar, with profits expected to be down 25–45 percent in 2009 compared with 2008 (McKinsey & Company 2009b). McKinsey cited falling revenues and limited cost controls as reasons for lower profit margins on both sides of the Atlantic.

Sources at recruitment firms also remarked that they expect a greater skewing of bonuses in favor of those who performed well, with the objective of motivating and retaining talent through a very difficult period.

Figure 8.1.   Profit Pool for Asset Management Firms in Western Europe, 2007–2009E

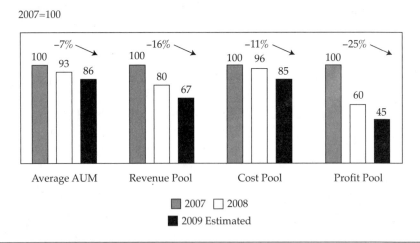

Source: Based on data from McKinsey & Company (2009a).

Godliman Partner's data relative to the U.K. market show that, prior to 2009, most remuneration was grouped in a fairly tight bell curve around the median, with second- and third-quartile ranges extending only around £50,000 up or down (that is, if the median was £249,000, then the majority of people would receive compensation of between £300,000 and £200,000). Godliman expects the bell curve to flatten substantially because in its view, a clear polarization between strong and weak performers now exists.

Stagnant to falling salaries on the buy side when the sell side is booming is creating some problems for asset management firms as they compete with the sell side for talent. A source at an executive search firm in the United States commented, "In general, total compensation for 2009 compared with 2008 is up on the sell side and down on the buy side. The sell side is booming, profitability is back, and firms are trying to figure out how to pay people without a public backlash. This situation creates a double problem for the buy side: euphoria on one side of [Wall] Street competing for talent, which puts the buy side at a disadvantage. The issue is expectations. Often the buy and sell sides move in tandem; now there is a very big mismatch."

An analysis of year-end incentives in the U.S. financial services sector by Johnson Associates, Inc. (2009), showed a similar picture. According to this New York–based compensation consultancy, year-end incentives are forecast to be up by 40 percent on average at investment and commercial banks and down by around 20 percent at asset management firms, alternative investment firms, and insurance companies (see **Figure 8.2**). Johnson's estimates are based on the firm's ongoing monitoring of the financial services industry and public data from 10 of the largest U.S. asset management and related service firms (A–J on the left side of the figure) and 8 of the largest U.S. investment and commercial banks (A–H on the right side of the figure). Projecting incentive trends in the future on the basis of past data from the same sampling—that is, 10 of the largest U.S. asset managers and related service firms and 8 of the largest U.S. investment and commercial banks—Johnson forecasts that 2010 bonuses at asset management firms will remain significantly lower than in 2007 (down 30 percent) whereas bonuses at banks will be only moderately below their 2007 level (down 7 percent) (see **Figure 8.3**).

If asset managers have found it difficult to compete with the sell side in attracting top talent, institutional investors managing assets in-house (traditionally paying even less) have often found it difficult to compete with the buy side for talent. But sources remarked that today's soft job market is making it easier for institutional investors to attract talent. A source at a large corporate pension fund that is bringing the management of more assets in-house in an attempt to gain better control and improve performance said, "Hiring and retaining talent is a major challenge. We have a special salary plan for remuneration, but before bringing assets in-house, we

Figure 8.2.   Projected Percentage Change in the Year-End Incentive Pool in Asset Management and Banking

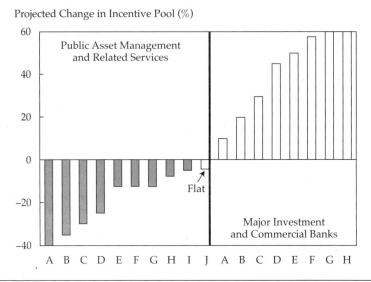

Note: Projections assume varying ability of firms to repay TARP (Troubled Asset Relief Program) capital; significant TARP recipients may be affected more broadly due to uncertainty surrounding pending legislation.

Source: Based on data from Johnson Associates, Inc. (2009, p. 3).

ask ourselves, do we have a plan to attract talent?" According to this source, the present environment is making it easier to attract people who would have been difficult to attract before: "We are now finding candidates not only at a lower price, but they are more viable. We don't pay hedge fund salaries, but we can now tap people who have left hedge funds."

In addition to trends in salaries, sources remarked that compensation is being reconsidered, with the objectives of retaining talent and/or achieving a better alignment of incentives with the long-term profitability of the firm. A source in the United Kingdom identified a growing use of deferred compensation as one of three major trends in the industry. The source remarked that asset management firms stand to gain: "The recent pressure by the U.K.'s Financial Services Authority [FSA] to defer a greater portion of the bonus award into some form of long-term incentive plan [LTIP] benefits the asset management firms because it helps lock staff into the firm. There has already been a recent trend in this direction. So, I would expect asset managers to make even greater use of deferral schemes in the future."

Figure 8.3. Incentive Trend 2007–2010 at U.S. Asset Management and Related Services Firms and Investment and Commercial Banks

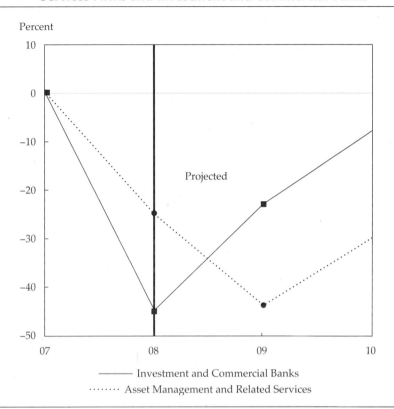

Source: Based on data from Johnson Associates, Inc. (2009, p. 4).

The Russell Reynolds report (2009) revealed that, as compensation structures are being reviewed, a larger percentage of compensation is being deferred, performance is being evaluated over a multiyear period, and incentives are being aligned with long-term profitability of, in some cases, the unit rather than the parent company.

Positions for Which Firms Are Recruiting

Sources in North America and Europe reported that recruitment searches are up for asset allocation specialists and for individuals with multi-asset experience and quantitative skills but down for stock pickers and, in general, for anyone on the equity side. A source from Germany said, "Professionals with a quantitative background are in high demand, along with specialists in asset allocation and multi-asset classes. There is also a demand for ETF specialists in sales, trading, and structuring."

A source in the United Kingdom said, "The demand for people with multi-asset-class experience is now high. Three to four years ago, the trend was for specialist mandates. Now we see the pendulum swinging to multi-asset classes. It is not exactly the old balanced mandates of the past, but there is now a lot of focus on absolute returns, and it is easier to do this if you can play across a range of asset classes."

Although sources noted that the demand for people with multi-asset-class experience is high, they observed that filling positions is not so easy. A recruiter in the United States remarked, "It is difficult to find qualified candidates for asset allocation. There are few people with hands-on experience in more than one asset class. It is even more difficult to find people with experience in portfolio construction and risk and liquidity issues in multi-asset classes. This aspect is now a big part of our recruiting missions."

Sources at recruitment firms said that early in 2009, they were busy recruiting fixed-income managers and analysts. This focus was a reflection of several things, including investor demand for fixed-income products in the first half of 2009, the reportedly poor performance of some fixed-income teams that were being replaced, and the failure of credit rating agencies.

A source in the United Kingdom noted, "There has been an increase in senior hiring in fixed income, which reflects the fact that a number of houses have brought in new management to address poor performance and overhaul investment processes; 2009 also saw an increased demand for fixed-income fund managers as investors switched out of risky assets."

A source at a recruitment firm in the United States remarked, "We have seen a lot of hiring of people with deep knowledge on the credit side as firms realized that they cannot trust the rating agencies. Many held AAA rated securities that were downgraded and, conversely, poorly rated securities doing better."

Recruiting activity in compliance functions was reported to be flat, whereas in the wake of the Lehman Brothers collapse and the Madoff and Galleon scandals, sources reported that demand outstripped supply in risk management, especially with operational and counterparty risk managers. As 2009 progressed and markets recouped losses, some demand emerged for asset servicers and gatherers in the institutional arena where the money is stickier.

A source in the United Kingdom said,

We have seen an increased demand for asset servicers in 2009 relative to previous years. In 2008, there was a more than 10 percent increase in the number of team leaders hired as firms overhauled their distribution efforts in response to the crisis. In 2009, with most of the senior hires in place, hiring has been more about in-filling. As the year progressed, a growing demand for asset gatherers occurred as confidence grew and firms moved on from their previously defensive stance.

Recruitment of retail wholesaling staff, however, was reported to be soft throughout 2009. Reasons cited include a decline in the open-architecture model and the high cost of retail distribution platforms amid shrinking revenues and margins. The latter is leading to a lot of consolidation in some markets.

A source in Germany identified sales professionals in mutual fund distribution as the professional profile least in demand in 2009. According to this source, "Recruitment of sales professionals in mutual fund distribution was down 50 percent in 2009 compared with 2008. Here in Germany, revenues in the retail market are shrinking, ETFs are in greater demand, and the open-architecture model is in decline at the banks."

A source in the United States remarked, "Retail distribution platforms looked very expensive in 2008. The only place where we are seeing some activity in retail is in marketing and in social networking. What we have seen is that whenever possible, asset managers are driving retail and mass affluent sales through the web."

Indeed, the Russell Reynolds report (2009) on trends in recruiting and compensation noted that firms reacted to a loss of assets and lower profit margins in the retail sector following the 2008 economic downturn by cutting up to 50 percent of their external wholesaling staffs.

Asset Classes in Which Firms Are Recruiting

According to sources, recruitment searches for the first half of 2009 were concentrated in the low-alpha, investment-grade product areas and especially in fixed income and money markets. Sources also noted, however, that with the equity markets up at midyear, the risk appetite of investors was coming back. By the third quarter of 2009, recruitment was up in the area of distressed debt and other distressed assets, such as private equity and real estate, and down in the money markets.

Speaking in the third quarter of 2009, a recruiter in the United Kingdom said, "The greatest hiring demand this year in fixed income has been lower down the risk curve for managers in government bonds and especially investment-grade credit. There has been little demand for higher-risk or higher-alpha areas—hence, the demand for people in high-yield and emerging-market debt has fallen."

A source in the United States concurred but noted that, more recently, demand has picked up for distressed assets: "There has been a lot of recruiting in fixed income in 2009, and we saw some activity for recruiting for distressed debt earlier in the year. That was low-hanging fruit. Now in the fourth quarter, we are seeing firms raising assets for other such distressed assets as private equity and real estate, with recruitment following."

Meanwhile, the growing popularity of real estate as an investment class is driving recruitment in Central Europe. A source from Germany said, "Demand has grown the most in real estate. The strongest push here was in institutional business as the demand for indirect real estate investments of institutional investors has grown over the past two years and further growth is expected. Searches were up 75 percent in 2009 compared with 2008."

As for where recruitment was the softest, sources identified equities, at least for the first half of 2009. A recruiter in the United States remarked, "Who did we recruit the least of? Stock pickers. We had hardly any missions for stock pickers in 2009. Will stock pickers come back? Yes, in certain strategies, such as smaller cap and emerging markets."

Indeed, some sources said that after all the hiring for distressed debt and credit that was so characteristic of 2008 and the first half of 2009, they were seeing a renewed demand for talent in global (outside of the United States) and emerging market equities. Still other sources perceived opportunistic hiring in equities, with firms hiring complete teams or managers with portable track records that they can easily assimilate and sell.

Who Was Hiring in 2009

Sources in North America and Europe reported that recruitment was up in 2009 compared with 2008 at asset management boutiques and insurance firms, whereas recruitment was down for the same period at large asset management and private equity firms and hedge funds.

A source at a recruitment firm in Germany said, "Throughout the first half of 2009, the large asset managers were making people redundant and only hired in exceptional cases. In general, search mandates in 2009 were dominated by smaller firms, such as investment boutiques and family offices. Professionals from larger organizations were frustrated or had lost their jobs and were willing to move to smaller organizations."

A source in the United States observed, "Insurance companies, such as the global players Allianz and the AXA Group, were among the most active recruiters in 2009 for general accounts and asset management subsidiaries. They seized the opportunity to attract some folks they would not normally have been able to attract." It was reported, however, that smaller insurance firms are reexamining their approach to asset management, with many deciding to outsource the function.

As for hedge funds and private equity, one source said, "There was almost no activity during the first half of 2009, although some buzz began in the third quarter."

Although sources at executive search firms that we talked to had no missions for institutional investors, many of the big institutional investors we talked to said that they are bringing more assets in-house (see Chapter 4) and increasing staff. While salaries might not match those at asset management firms, the job comes with less stress. A source at a large U.K. pension fund commented, "One benefit of managing assets in-house is a sense of stability of the client relationship, especially in difficult times. We can nurture talent rather than take a hire-and-fire approach. We have noted that external managers are more stressed about performance—they systematically use up all the risk tolerance the firm has—whereas internal teams rarely get close to the risk tolerance of the firm."

Professional Qualifications in Demand

Professional qualifications most in demand in 2009 were the masters of business administration (MBA) or the equivalent European business school degree as well as the CFA designation or a European equivalent. Although the CFA designation has long been in demand in North America, its appeal is more recent in Europe.

A source at a recruitment firm in the United States said, "There is no change here—CFA designations and MBAs have been the requirement for a long time. It might vary from firm to firm. Some prefer the CFA designation; others prefer MBAs, or vice versa. But it is important that the candidate demonstrates that he or she is committed to a career in asset management. A way to demonstrate that commitment is to continue to educate oneself."

A recruiter in the United Kingdom remarked, "In my view, the CFA designation is gaining in importance. It has become a basic qualification without which younger professionals will find it difficult to progress. Our U.S. clients routinely favor candidates with the CFA [designation] over those without, although U.K. clients tend to give it less weighting."

A source at a Swiss private bank said,

> Asset managers must gear up to advise clients on, for example, asset allocation and their macroeconomic views. We are increasing the knowledge base required for employees. For example, we now require that the institutional sales people have the CFA [designation]. We see some big banks are reducing qualifications to bring costs down because they want to get rid of high-paid private bankers that do not have university degrees. These banks have bloated costs. But that is the wrong way to go even if, in the short term, it might look good. Clients are getting more information, they are getting smarter, and they are asking more questions. Five to ten years ago, the private investor knew what a stock was, what a bond was, and not much more. Now, information flows more freely. If you reduce qualifications here, clients might end up being more knowledgeable than their private bankers are.

Employment Outlook for 2010

Sources at recruitment firms in North America and Europe expect searches in the asset and wealth management industry to be up in 2010 compared with 2009. This evaluation is based on the belief that markets will stabilize and continue to recoup losses throughout 2010. Employment in the sector is, sources remarked, market driven.

A source in the United States said, "We expect recruiting missions to be up moderately in 2010 but not back to 2007–2008 levels. Some firms are already thinking about putting out searches in the fourth quarter to have people on board in the first quarter of 2010."

A source in Germany said, "We expect to have 25 percent more search mandates in 2010 compared with 2009, and this after being down 50 percent in 2009 compared with 2008. But the asset management job market will not come back to the level of 2007 in 2010. The industry will continue to restructure, adapt to the changed market situation, and consolidate. Ongoing and upcoming mergers will reduce the number of job openings and, in the case of a merger, will freeze headcounts until the integration is finalized."

Future Opportunities

We asked sources to identify where future opportunities exist in the industry. The areas most frequently mentioned were asset allocation and multi-asset-class management. A source in the United States said, "We expect future job opportunities to be in asset allocation—the demand is high, and it is always hard to find qualified persons."

A U.S. asset manager added, "A new area on the portfolio manager side that is starting to emerge but is currently only a speck on the horizon is managing multiple portfolios within a single portfolio of, for example, marketable securities. The portfolio is run as a unit with various asset classes, like a jigsaw puzzle. It is similar to the old balanced mandates but is not the same thing. It is a collection of focus funds under one umbrella, with an array of possible investments, such as government bonds, corporate bonds, and equities."

Other areas frequently mentioned that present new opportunities include global and emerging-markets equities, renewable resources, socially responsible investing (SRI), real estate, commodities, and higher-risk fixed income. A source at a recruitment firm in Germany said, "We expect a restructuring of the industry and innovation on the product side. We are seeing demand for roles within renewables, commodities, real estate, SRI, multi-asset-class solutions, quantitative asset management, and asset allocation. There will also be demand for people in asset/liability management [ALM] and liability-driven investment [LDI]."

An investment consultant in Germany remarked that demand for analysts will grow in areas other than equity. According to this source, "New alternative asset classes will require analysts in such areas as infrastructure (as government money is pumped into schools and roads), in private equity, in real estate (which will turn out to be one of the best asset classes in the near term), in forestry, in commodities (including metals), in soft commodities, and in socially responsible investments."

Sources remarked that a shortage currently exists of persons with such skills. A source at a large Canadian pension fund said, "There is a growing role for analysts in alternative asset classes, such as infrastructure, real estate, and private equity, but it is difficult to find people adequately trained in these asset classes. We have to train them ourselves in-house."

Another growth area for jobs in asset management is in risk management, with both asset managers and consultants. A source at a recruitment firm said, "There will be future job opportunities in counterparty risk as a result of Lehman Brothers' collapse and as a better recourse to outsourcing and in operational risk as a result of scandals, such as Madoff and Galleon."

An investment consultant in the United States remarked, "There are job opportunities in risk management, operational due diligence, and compliance. It might be expensive, but if you look at performance and at oversight differentials, it is a small dip in the bucket compared with a potential loss."

Derivatives were identified as another growth area as pension funds and other institutional investors increase their use of these instruments. A source at the investment management arm of a large U.K. insurer remarked, "The growing demand for persons with experience in derivatives and overlays is related to the growth of absolute-return strategies and LDI. We have grown our in-house expertise of derivatives over the past two years. Knowledge of derivatives is now an important criterion in evaluating new hires."

Sources agreed that there will be fewer opportunities for portfolio managers and analysts in traditional asset management. A headhunter in Germany said, "Job opportunities will shrink in the traditional asset classes. The market is competitive and, therefore, a low-margin business. Investors today tend to invest in ETFs or passive asset management products for global or European investments but try to add return by investing in satellite, niche, or nontraditional investments. Additionally, successful asset allocation is seen as the larger performance driver than single stock picking."

An investment consultant based in Germany concurred. According to this source, "If passive management goes up—and I think that it will go up—there will be less value for active equity managers, so the demand for fundamental analysts in equities will be down."

A source at a Swiss private bank added, "Active management is now perceived as a commodity that destroys rather than creates value. Job opportunities are down for anyone involved in active equity in developed markets, whether they are portfolio managers, analysts, or in sales. For example, in Luxembourg, the number of funds has been drastically reduced as banks close down a lot of funds that are no longer profitable."

Nevertheless, some sources noted that there will always be a need for good equity analysts, although they might not be concentrated on the sell side. Indeed, many asset managers continue to consider in-house analysis their unique selling proposition (USP).

A source at a large firm said,

> Definitely, a need for fundamental analysts exists, but the trend is away from sell-side analysts to buy-side analysts. Public information in copious amounts is available to all. Information has become a free good. But while analysts on the sell side must make information available to all, asset managers can have proprietary insight. They do not have to give their information to nonclients. The question is, Can asset managers afford to grow research teams? If you are Fidelity Investments, yes; if you are small and specialized, yes; if you are in the middle, you get squeezed.

Others sources, especially in continental Europe, believe that equity analysts will likely see their mandate become larger. A source at a northern European multiemployer pension fund said, "There is still a job for persons who look at cash flows, but there is a growing need for analysts who look at nonfinancial aspects, such as the environment or governance."

A source at an industrywide pension fund in the Netherlands concurred. According to this source, "There is so much sell-side research available, but in the future we will see more and better analysts on the buy side. They will be inside large pension funds, in areas such as corporate governance, environmental issues, alternative energy sources, macro environment, and policy issues. Research is now dominated by the portfolio manager who has a research team. But there are many things that are worthwhile to research other than the balance sheet of listed firms. We need to move to a higher level with research."

A source at a large U.K. pension fund concurred: "We have to up the quality of the analysis."

Regarding fixed income, sources were divided about whether job opportunities in the sector will increase or decline. A source in the United Kingdom that believes opportunities will decline remarked,

> Demand for fixed-income analysts has fallen. It is my feeling that there will continue to be lower demand for fixed-income analysts in the future. There had been sustained demand over the last five years to build up teams of seven or eight sector analysts. This demand was driven by investment consultants. When investment-grade spreads were low, however, analysts failed to generate any alpha; and when the markets fell, they failed to avoid the credit blowups. Hence, one might ask what purpose such large teams serve. My own view is that we will revert to a model in which each house has only two or three fixed-income analysts, tasked with coming up with "best picks" trading ideas.

Others, however, believe that, given the fact that one cannot rely on the credit rating agencies, asset and wealth managers will have to build up their own teams of fixed-income analysts. One source said, "Fundamental analysis is our USP, not only in equities but also in credit, where we have 20 analysts working in three locations. Given that the rating agencies have done such a poor job, we will be growing our credit analyst team."

In the future, demand is expected to remain strong for proven asset gatherers. A source in the United Kingdom commented, "Demand for distribution roles already picked up in the third quarter of 2009, and there is a lot of work in progress, which will register in the hiring stats in the first quarter of 2010. I think there will be continuing midlevel demand for U.K. asset gatherers and, on the continent, for Central European—for example, Germany, Austria, and Switzerland—and possibly Nordic specialists. This demand will be in line with asset managers' increased confidence in the economic recovery."

A headhunter in the United States added, "There are opportunities for institutional sales people. Everyone wants someone talented with great relationships and strong sales people who understand the products and the strategies."

Several sources pointed to the "retailization" of the industry as defined-benefit (DB) plans close and fuel demand for life insurance products, such as annuities in defined-contribution (DC) and mutual funds. The distributor will replace the pension plan sponsor as the wholesaler. One source remarked, "There will be a demand for people working in distribution, for example, someone who can raise US$2 billion in Japan through large distributors of financial products. The business will remain wholesale, but the wholesale client will be different. It will no longer be the CIO of the pension fund but the professional buyer of a distributor with 100,000 clients. This change will require a good relationship with large distributors and a knowledge of very different products."

More generally, the expectation is that fewer job opportunities will be available for middle managers who are not close to the revenue-generating lines of the business. "Fewer opportunities will exist in the future for middle management roles that are seen as costly to the business," one recruiter commented. This source further advised, "It is important for people to keep close to revenue lines."

In addition to jobs at asset and wealth management firms, a source at a U.S. investment consultancy said that opportunities are opening in consulting. According to this source,

> Top-tier investment consulting firms will have to increase the staff and expertise on their research teams to be able to research hedge funds, including operational risk, private equity, real estate, and commodity managers. Given the job situation, it is now not hard to find the expertise as people leave hedge funds, private equity, and so forth, and try to reposition themselves. We are seeing consulting firms hire former hedge fund managers and former private equity managers to research these

categories of managers. Career opportunities are opening because consultants must build and maintain truly professional staff. They have not traditionally done a good job in this area as they were competing with the investment management industry for jobs. But now a lot of people are getting out of investment management and moving into consulting.

Exhibit 8.1 summarizes where job opportunities are up and where they are down in investment management.

Exhibit 8.1. Employment Trends As Identified by Sources

What Is Up	What Is Down
• Asset allocation skills/multi-asset experience for absolute return mandates	• Portfolio managers, analysts, and sales in traditional asset management
• Quant skills/risk managers	• Stock pickers
• ETF specialists	• Mutual funds sales staff and retail wholesale staff
• Fixed-income managers, analysts	• Middle managers not close to revenue lines
• Distressed debt/high-risk fixed income	
• Operational/counterparty risk managers	
• Global (non-U.S.)/emerging-markets equities	
• SRI/infrastructure/renewable-resources portfolio managers, analysts	
• Derivatives experts in portfolio management, sales, trading	
• ALM/LDI experts	
• Analysts for alternative asset classes	
• Portfolio managers in alternatives, especially real estate and commodities	
• Asset servicers, gatherers	
• Retail web marketing	

Getting Back to Pre-Crisis Job Levels

Sources agreed that employment in the asset and wealth management industry in North America and Europe will not come back to pre-crisis levels before the second half of 2010 or 2011, if ever. Sources cited the fact that the headcount in the industry is down dramatically compared with its high-water mark in early 2007.

A source in the United Kingdom remarked, "Assuming that the markets continue to not decline, and barring any market shocks, I would expect employment in the industry as a whole to return to pre-crisis job levels sometime after the second or third quarter 2010. Most firms are still wary of the future, and I do not think there will be a strong return to hiring until the economic outlook is clearer."

A recruiter in Germany said, "The industry as a whole will get back to pre-crisis job levels in 2011. The asset management industry will be consolidating until then, as the larger asset managers and 'stuck-in-the-middle' asset managers merge. But, at the same time, new investment ideas will be developed and new investment boutiques will be established, so the overall demand will not decline."

112

A source at a recruitment firm in the United States added,

I do not know when the industry as a whole will get back to pre-crisis job levels, but it will not be fast. Firms would rather increase people's workloads before hiring. The industry has shrunk dramatically since the beginning of 2008. If I had to put a figure to it, I would say employment is down 30 percent. Firms were sized for handling more assets than they are now handling. They are rethinking and redefining their business model and considering outsourcing for functions, such as platforms and technology. We will see more consolidation. Many firms big and small were built for assets the firms no longer have. We might never get back to past job levels. Most firms have not recouped their losses on the profitability side, and most investors have not recouped their losses. If assets went down 50 percent, they would need to go up 100 percent to recoup losses.

An investment consultant in the United States shared the doubt that employment in the asset and wealth management industry will get back to pre-crisis levels. According to this source, "Going forward, there will be fewer jobs in traditional asset management because money will go to passive management. Employment in the industry may have hit a high-water mark; we will likely see some contraction in the industry."

It is interesting to note that Russell Reynolds's 2009 report on recruiting and compensation trends in the industry remarked that, following the recent market turbulence, the premise that asset and wealth management firms could manage other people's money without putting the firm's own capital at risk has been challenged. It foresees the need for business models and compensation paradigms to evolve.

A source at a private bank in Switzerland commented, "Given what happened in 2008, many clients are asking, Why pay for active management when performance was so poor? We have a good cost-to-income ratio, not because of high fees on the client—we are on the lower end here. Rather, we have controlled remuneration. We have never paid the highest salaries or the highest bonuses. We have a partnership structure. We do not get rich in the short term. There are no salary excesses, but over the long term, it is possible to make good money."[28]

Even if employment trends were to remain somewhat sluggish throughout 2010, a source at a large international executive recruitment firm said, "I would definitely advise graduates to go into the investment management industry. It is intellectually and financially rewarding."

---

[28]Interestingly, Jefferies & Company, Inc. (2007), remarked that an analysis of U.S. mutual fund companies reveals a link between direct employee ownership and the proportion of assets in buy-rated funds.

9. Looking Ahead

In the preceding chapters, we discussed what the industry identified as challenges in the post-crisis period. An underlying issue for all players is to define the promise of the investment management industry, whether it is to individual investors, members of pension plans, or foundations. Although our industry sources did not agree on just what the promise is—for example, to generate outperformance, to deliver absolute returns, or to optimize risk relative to returns—asset allocation and risk management are central to the job. The old split in which market risk was considered the investor's and benchmark risk the asset manager's is clearly no longer satisfactory to investors who have seen their assets tumble twice in a decade. In this chapter, we look at portfolio management theory, which is at the heart of asset allocation, and then at risk management, in which the objective is to determine the level of risk for the purpose of risk budgeting.

This Time Is Different

In the aftermath of the market turmoil of 2007–2009, risk managers, asset managers, and the economic profession at large were criticized for failing to foresee the crisis. But as one source commented, "When things go wrong, really wrong, just about everyone is complicit." Investors were asking for double-digit returns in an economy experiencing single-digit growth; the industry was being paid to generate those returns. Was the market crash foreseeable?

To begin answering this question, consider the history of financial crises. Minsky (1986) was one of the first to analyze the dynamics of crises in loosely regulated capitalistic systems. According to Minsky's analysis, financial crises are endemic to loosely regulated systems because markets over- and undershoot relative to the underlying economy. Unregulated systems generate an excess of credit in periods of economic prosperity and growth. This excess credit produces unsustainable economic and financial bubbles that eventually crash, with a sudden and severe contraction of market values and economic activity.

Classical finance theory has to some extent operated in an economic void, treating financial markets as if they are rational and infinitely deep. Infinite rational markets do not need to follow the underlying economy because, according to the theory, resources available for arbitrage are infinite and any economically meaningful difference between price and value will be removed by some (to be determined) agent. But from time to time, we are reminded that financial markets cannot grow indefinitely at a rate that is greater than the rate of economic growth of their respective regions without the need for realignment.

114

More recently, Reinhart and Rogoff (2008) analyzed major financial crises in 66 countries over a period of 800 years. The surprising finding is that these crises had much in common: the accumulation of debt, inflation, a banking crisis, and, frequently, an origin in financial centers. Using ample historical evidence to demonstrate the patterns and consequences of crises, Reinhart and Rogoff showed that financial and banking crises exhibit similar patterns in mature and emerging markets alike. Based on their historical analysis, they concluded that, in 2007, ". . . standard indicators for the United States, such as asset price inflation, rising leverage, large sustained current account deficits, and a slowing trajectory of economic growth, exhibited virtually all the signs of a country on the verge of a financial crisis—indeed, a severe one."

Reinhart and Rogoff observed that, in general, the aftermath of a severe financial crisis has three characteristics. They wrote that:

> . . . the aftermath of severe financial crises share three characteristics. First, asset market collapses are deep and prolonged. Real housing price declines average 35 percent stretched out over six years, while equity price collapses average 55 percent over a downturn of about three and a half years. Second, the aftermath of banking crises is associated with profound declines in output and employment. The unemployment rate rises an average of 7 percentage points over the down phase of the cycle, which lasts on average over four years. Output falls (from peak to trough) an average of over 9 percent, although the duration of the downturn, averaging roughly two years, is considerably shorter than for unemployment. Third, the real value of government debt tends to explode, rising an average of 86 percent in the major post–World War II episodes.

Interestingly, the authors found that although bank bailouts involve a huge amount of money, the major driver of government debt is the collapse in tax revenues caused by a deep and prolonged contraction of economic activity.

In the United States, the rate of growth of financial profits is well above the rate of growth of the nation's overall GDP—a signal of an approaching financial crisis—and is reflected in the financial sector's share of all U.S. corporate profits. In the third quarter of 2009, according to economist Dean Baker, co-director of the Center for Economic and Policy Research in Washington, DC, financial firms accounted for 34 percent of all U.S. corporate profits. This inordinate share of corporate profits suggests that either inefficiencies existed in the financial system able to generate very large profits or sources existed of paper profit not rooted in the economy itself but related to other factors—for example, to the process of money generation that creates asset inflation.

According to Minsky's (1986) analysis, the second explanation is more likely because an excess of credit and money is ultimately responsible for an excess of financial profit. Leverage itself has a role in financial crises in that it creates asset inflation. At the onset of the most recent crisis, the amount of leverage in the economy was unknown. Roger Ibbotson, professor of finance at Yale School of Management, comments, "It is important to know how much leverage is out there; it is not always reported in a way that makes it intelligible. When volatility is low, you can take on a lot of leverage, but when volatility rises, you need to bring the leverage down. In mid-2007, a lot of firms shifted leverage down to bring volatility down, thereby creating a dip in the price of the assets they themselves owned."

Now consider the methods of money management. If investors and the investment management industry must indeed learn how to better protect assets from recurrent market turmoil, we might need to revisit portfolio theory and risk management. We will begin our discussion with a reappraisal of modern portfolio theory.

Revisiting Modern Portfolio Theory

When all the major stock markets crashed in 2008–2009, diversification and risk management seemed to have failed. Many asked if modern portfolio theory (MPT) needed to be revisited. First formulated in the 1950s primarily by Harry Markowitz, who was later awarded the Nobel Prize in Economic Science for his work, MPT is not a theory in the philosophical sense but a set of prescriptions about how investors should allocate their resources.[29]

In its initial formulation, MPT assumes that risk can be measured by the variance of returns (σ^2) and that investors should allocate resources by making an optimal trade-off between risk and return. In the original formulation, the trade-off is represented by a penalty term, $1/2A\sigma^2$, by which investors could maximize utility by holding the portfolio with the highest expected return after subtracting the penalty: $\max[E(r) - 1/2A\sigma^2]$. The estimation of the expected return and the variance for any portfolio is key to MPT. MPT can be applied *if* expected returns and all the needed moments can be estimated. Asset prices need not follow a random walk. MPT is compatible with dynamic pricing theories and models. In the presence of transaction costs or consumption streams, basic MPT might not be optimal and a multiperiod version of MPT might be needed.

Academics we talked to challenged the view that MPT failed in the recent financial crisis. Professor Ibbotson said,

> I think that the idea that diversification failed during the 2007–2009 crisis is completely wrong. In 2008, bonds—at least high-quality bonds—were up while most equity markets fell together. But the idea of diversification, properly understood, is between the three major asset classes—stocks, bonds, and cash. And, as I said, stocks were down but high-quality bonds were up, although low-quality

---

[29]Note that the term "MPT" is sometimes used to refer to a theory in the philosophical sense that incorporates the work of not only Harry Markowitz but also Merton Miller, Franco Modigliani, William Sharpe, James Tobin, Jack Treynor, Fischer Black, and others. In this monograph, we use MPT in a restricted sense.

bonds were down. Actually, the correlation between stocks and high-quality bonds went to near zero. Cash was stable throughout. There is another aspect of diversification, at the level of individual stocks. Throughout the crisis, holding individual stocks was much more volatile than holding funds. In 2008, almost 25 percent of U.S. stocks lost 75 percent of their value but only four out of 66,000 open-ended mutual funds lost that much. Holding a mutual fund is much less risky than holding individual stocks.

Yu Zhu, a professor at the China Europe International Business School, cited a study by Bartram and Bodnar (2009) that showed that although all equity markets did indeed go down by 40–50 percent from 31 December 2007 to 27 February 2009, stocks of some industrial sectors suffered larger losses than other sectors. For example, for the same period, U.S. financials were down 71 percent. Professor Zhu concluded, "A portfolio concentrated in financials would have done much worse than a broadly diversified portfolio."

Stephen Schaefer, professor of finance at London Business School, commented, "When people suggest that modern portfolio theory has outlived its usefulness, it is not clear exactly what they are saying: That we would actually be better off not trying to measure risk and return? It is true that a naive application of MPT is not useful, but in my experience, people do not use MPT mechanically. Sensible, thoughtful, and constructive use of MPT informs decisions rather than makes them."

MPT is a broad paradigm, and one needs to distinguish the paradigm from its implementations. Consider, for example, the question of the nonnormality of returns. If asset returns are normally distributed, classical MPT requires estimating the variance and the expected return of each asset and the covariances for each pair of assets. If returns are not normally distributed, higher moments must also be estimated. Higher moments describe the asymmetries and the fat-tailed behavior of distributions. The need to estimate higher moments is not explicit in MPT. If, for whatever reason, investors are not concerned with asymmetries and fat tails, MPT requires an estimation of only expected returns, variances, and covariances. In evaluating the usefulness of MPT, we must distinguish between the following three possible uses of the term: (1) the general principle of optimizing the expected utility of the investor at a given time horizon, (2) any specific form of the utility function, and (3) any specific form of the estimators used for expected returns, variances, covariances, and any other inputs that the utility function might require.

First, we will discuss estimation issues. Expected returns, variances, covariances, and higher moments are usually estimated based on past returns. Even assuming that returns are a sequence of independent and identically distributed variables (i.e., that prices follow a random or stochastic walk), estimating returns, variances, and covariances is a formidable task subject to a large number of small-sample errors. In fact, in estimating expected returns, we effectively estimate stochastic (not true) trends.

As proved by Merton (1980), variances and covariances can be estimated more accurately than expected returns from the same time series. In practice, long series of returns are needed to estimate expected returns (some analysts rely on forward-looking measures, such as a dividend discount model for equities, but forecasting discounted dividends still requires long histories of past data). Estimating variances and covariances, however, is made difficult by the fact that the number of entries in a variance–covariance matrix grows with the square of the number of return series whereas available data grow only linearly with the number of series. For example, consider an aggregate such as the S&P 500. With four years of weekly data, there are 1,000 data points for each stock return series and thus a total of 500,000 data points. The variance–covariance matrix of the S&P 500 includes 500 × 499/2 = 124,750 independent entries. Therefore, approximately only four data points are produced per estimate. To estimate the Russell 1000 covariance matrix, twice as many data points exist—that is, one million data points—but four times more entries need to be estimated—that is, there are 1,000 × 999/2 = 499,500 entries, but only two data points per estimate.

Dimensionality reduction techniques are necessary. To estimate higher-order moments to account for fat tails (i.e., extreme events), even more radical simplifications need to be applied as the number of third- and fourth-order moments grows with the third or fourth power of the number of time series.

MPT is a single-period framework, but as mentioned earlier, it does not depend on the assumption that prices follow random walks. MPT simply requires a forecast of expected returns and moments at each point in time. If dynamic models of returns are adopted, all the parameters of a dynamic model need to be estimated—a significantly more difficult estimation task. Again, dimensionality reduction techniques and simplifications are needed.

What can realistically be achieved with MPT? The classical version of MPT is clearly outdated. It is well known that marketwide correlations exist, that limits to diversification exist, and that the resulting optimized portfolio will still exhibit a risk that is dependent on the market and that might result in substantial losses (this statement is, in fact, a fairly good summary of the capital asset pricing model of William Sharpe [1964] and others). MPT, however, is an adaptable framework.

The advances of MPT in its first 50 years were summarized in Fabozzi, Gupta, and Markowitz (2002). But as observed by Professor Zhu, in the following decade the world was hit by a very large financial crisis. MPT does not offer the promise of eliminating losses—even large losses—even under the most favorable assumptions. John Finnerty, professor and director of the Master of Science in Quantitative Finance Program at Fordham University, commented, "Diversification didn't fail. While it did not prevent losses, portfolios that were poorly diversified by being very heavily overweighted in equities lost more than well-diversified portfolios. Diversification cannot prevent losses; it can only mitigate them."

Perhaps the most important lesson learned is that all the relevant parameters, including correlations and expected returns, are time varying. Allan Timmermann, professor of finance at the University of California, San Diego, commented, "For short-run allocation purposes, it is clear that means correlations and variances change dramatically over time. Therefore, the model needs to be taught in its 'conditional' version with time-varying estimates of means and covariances. For longer horizons, the jury is still deciding, but there do seem to be shifts in how asset returns correlate across decades. Witness a shift in bond–stock correlations in 1998." Ilmanen (2003) analyzed the determinants of correlations between bonds and stocks and updated the data on stock–bond correlations for 1890–2010 (see **Figure 9.1**). The illustration shows that the correlation is generally positive but turned negative in eight periods, and it is now close to zero.

What really happened is still the subject of debate. Earlier studies—for example, Longin and Solnik (2001)—found that correlations increase in times of crisis. But in times of crisis, returns are not normally distributed but present fat tails (i.e., the probability of large events is much larger than it is in a normal distribution). Professor Ibbotson remarked, "Of course, one should think of returns not only as a normal distribution but also in various and different ways—for example, different

Figure 9.1. Evolution of the Correlation between Stocks and Bonds for 1890–2010

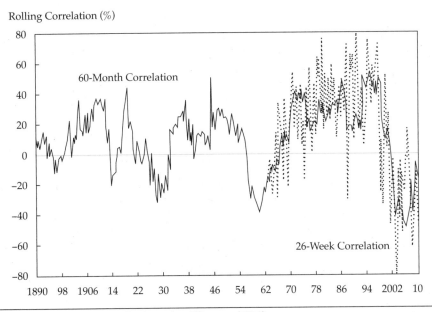

Source: Data kindly provided by Professor Antti Ilmanen (2003).

types of distributions by using Monte Carlo analysis. Outlier types of events perhaps need to be given more emphasis. Some of these distributions are asymmetrical, but we have the tools to measure them." It has been suggested that what appears as an increase in correlation is, in fact, a fat tail.[30] In the presence of fat tails, linear correlations do not work; concepts such as copula functions must be used.

The market crashes of 2000 and 2008 cannot be considered instances of the failure of diversification or the failure of MPT. There is no support in MPT for the claim that diversification produces a steady stream of positive returns. As Jonathan Berk, professor of finance at Stanford University, remarked, "What is true, and was known before 2008, is that stocks move together in big crashes, so the benefit of diversification is less in crashes. But that does not mean that there is no benefit to diversification or that investors should not diversify."

An optimized portfolio can produce negative returns, even a stream of negative returns, purely by chance. But the crashes of 2000 and 2008 witnessed a long sequence of negative returns in excess of what could be expected simply by chance. The key points are that (1) MPT and diversification cannot mitigate the consequences of severe bear markets and that (2) current forecasting methods might not be adequate for predicting a forthcoming crisis.

The simultaneous negative behavior of many asset classes is not a failure of diversification but a reversal of trends; in prior time periods, all the asset classes went up together. Stock index levels, as measured by the S&P 500, dropped 57 percent from the peak of 2007 to the trough of March 2009. This type of behavior is not a failure of cross-sectional diversification but involves other phenomena, such as the inversion of trends and a change in the pricing of risk. Stock and government bond returns were negatively correlated for almost 16 months.

Diversification and Alternatives

In addition to using the three traditional asset classes—stocks, bonds, and cash—for diversification purposes, investors are increasingly turning to alternative asset classes that, depending on the country and context, might refer to, among others, hedge funds, private equity, real estate, hard and soft commodities, foreign exchange, or less tangible assets such as intellectual property rights. We asked academics how they evaluated the contribution of these asset classes to outperformance and diversification strategies. Generally, academics we talked to are skeptical about why the price behavior of these asset classes would be different from public assets. Guofu Zhou, professor of finance at Washington University, commented that although some alternatives may be good, caution is required; hedge funds, for example, might not hedge at all what one wants hedged.

---

[30]See Campbell, Forbes, Koedijk, and Kofman (2008).

Professor Schaefer added,

Many people claim that there is evidence of systematically superior performance in alternative asset classes. But it is important to remember that although we hear a lot about success stories, such as the Harvard and Yale endowments, we hear much less about the failures, and it is very difficult for people to correct their judgment for this selection bias. The evidence overall is very sketchy. Take hedge funds: Arriving at a good estimate of average hedge fund performance is quite difficult because it requires identifying correctly the relevant population of hedge funds at a given time in the past. Databases of this kind exist for mutual funds, but for hedge funds it's more difficult.

In a study done for the Norwegian Government Pension Fund, Ang, Goetzmann, and Schaefer (2009) wrote, ". . . there is little convincing evidence of superior risk-adjusted returns to private equity and venture capital. Although some studies suggest skill persistence, the current data are not conclusive on this point. In the real estate sector, there is simply not enough information to evaluate whether managers have added value on a risk-adjusted basis."

Professors Timmermann and Ibbotson commented on the role of liquidity in achieving effective diversification with alternative asset classes. Professor Timmermann observed, "Even alternatives need liquidity, so it is not clear that their prices will not also plummet during periods of crisis. The key question is when and how much liquidity is needed by asset managers." Professor Ibbotson added, "Alternatives are generally good for diversification and probably offer decent returns but are quite illiquid and might tie up capital for long periods of time. Pension funds usually have long time horizons, but (in the last crisis) plans and endowments, such as Harvard and Stanford, needed cash and found that they could not get out of their alternatives. It was a problem of not having recognized the amount of liquidity needed."

Academics also questioned the assumption of the greater price stability of nonpublicly traded assets. Professor Timmermann remarked, "If (one invests in nonpublic assets and) these assets aren't liquid, it is not clear that it will help stabilize asset values. What was the value of a timber investment during 2008–2009? It is not clear that the price of this type of investment was not equally badly affected by the crisis." Professor Ibbotson added, "It is kind of like if one holds stocks and does not read the *Wall Street Journal*: You do not have price information, so you do not see the price changes."

Professor Berk summed up the academic skepticism about the contribution of nonpublic assets to the level and stability of returns by saying, "As an academic, it is hard to understand why nonpublicly traded assets would not be subject to the same shocks as publicly traded assets. So I do not understand why such a strategy would be effective."

Managing Assets Dynamically

It has escaped no one's attention that funds holding a high percentage of bonds outperformed funds holding a high percentage of stocks in 2008. The perception that the asset mix, not the specific securities held, and the ability to switch in and out of asset classes largely determine returns is behind the adoption of dynamic asset allocation, which has been adopted by some funds and is incorporated (to some degree) in some defined-contribution plans. Academics we talked to are generally skeptical that asset managers had the forecasting capability necessary to allow successful market timing.

Professor Schaefer remarked,

> Evidence of consistently successful dynamic asset allocation is very thin. In stressed market conditions, such as in the crisis we have just been through, prices in many markets—and credit markets in particular—were clearly far from their fundamental value, and investors who were able to supply liquidity at these times received a significant premium. This scenario is dynamic asset allocation of a kind, but in most cases, investors who were able to profit from these conditions owed more to fund structure, particularly the absence of leverage, than to superior forecasting ability.

Professor Ibbotson, suggesting that the ability to time markets is easier if working with subsets rather than whole asset classes, said,

> It has always been difficult to time the markets, but it is easier to time parts of the market—for example, large cap versus small cap or individual securities. I have seen very little evidence to support the fact that people are successful at timing their allocation between broad asset classes, but the more finely you cut it, the easier it is to do market timing. One piece of evidence that subsets are able to outperform comes from a study on hedge funds (Ibbotson, Chen, and Zhu, forthcoming 2011); the study shows that whole classes of investors are able to perform even after high fees. Among these are especially the global macro funds.

Another piece of evidence that market timing can be done successfully on subsets is the existence of cross-autocorrelations between sectors—for example, between size-sorted portfolios. (Cross-autocorrelation is the correlation between the value of one time series and the *lagged* value of another.) This event was demonstrated by Kanas and Kouretas (2005), who found that, in general, large-cap stocks are price leaders whereas small-cap stocks are price followers.

Commenting on the forecasting ability of the profession, however, and its impact on the ability to generate returns, Professor Ibbotson remarked, "Beating the market is a zero-sum game. For one to outperform, there must be someone that underperforms the market. Some subsets do well. But it is not due to a modeling trick or to extrapolation methods but rather to a combination of things, including better judgment, better information, better modeling, and more speed in execution."

Revisiting Risk Management

Industry sources identified risk management as the area most changed by the recent market turmoil. We asked academics how they evaluated our assessment of the need for managing risk and the tools for doing so. Generally, academics agreed about the need to pay more attention to the tails of the distributions, to consider liquidity risk more carefully, to better understand the interplay between different types of risks, and to consider systemic risk.

Professor Timmermann remarked, "Allowing for separate sources of risk—where these are usually bundled into one single component—is very important in future work. Liquidity risk introduces higher correlation across assets, and so it should be emphasized in particular. Usually we take risk parameters as fixed, but they clearly are subject to change. Risk monitoring measures that allow us to predict spikes in the risk parameters are clearly needed." Specific to tail events, he added, "The theory is already there, but it is difficult to estimate precisely the tails of return distributions. Estimation risk needs to be emphasized more."

Now, we will discuss the separate sources of risk along with ways of measuring and eventually hedging against them.

Liquidity Risk

"The crisis has reminded us of the critical importance of liquidity risk, and," commented Professor Schaefer, "it's both a blessing and a curse that these reminders arrive so infrequently. The pricing differential between liquid and illiquid assets that emerged in the crisis was very large and evident both between markets—for example, between the corporate and government bond markets—and within markets—for example, between on- and off-the-run government bonds." Professor Finnerty identified the need to incorporate liquidity considerations as the one area in which MPT does need to be refined. According to Professor Finnerty, "We need to take into account the possibility that the financial system can experience periods of extraordinary illiquidity. Relative liquidity is an important investment attribute, but we need better methods of measuring the value of a security's liquidity and the value security liquidity contributes to portfolio value. Credit derivatives provide an effective means of hedging credit risk and furnishing credit risk pricing, but we don't have anything analogous for liquidity risk, although I suspect that such instruments will be developed."

Professor Ibbotson emphasized the need to consider liquidity on a continuum as opposed to putting entire asset classes into preconceived liquidity buckets. He observed, "We can monitor liquidity risk, do scenario analysis, ask how much liquidity we need and how much liquidity the assets have in different situations. But people put things into buckets; they say stocks are liquid and private equity is illiquid. In reality, there are gradations of liquidity in each category. Liquidity needs to be managed in both public and private markets."

As for hedging liquidity risk, Professor Schaefer remarked, "No obvious ways to hedge liquidity risk exist that can be relied on to work well across markets. Because major liquidity shocks arrive only infrequently, there is relatively little data on which to test how well or how badly a hedge might perform. It also seems likely that the impact of liquidity shocks is strongly nonlinear (i.e., a given shock may have a substantially different impact according to the state of the economy)."

Fat Tails

Intuitively, a probability distribution is said to have fat tails if the probability associated with the tails of the distribution is larger than the tails in the Gaussian (normal) case. If a probability distribution is fat tailed, large events, such as large market movements, are more likely to occur than would be the case if the phenomenon could be described by a normal distribution. The difference can be economically important. For example, a return with a magnitude six times the standard deviation of the distribution would be practically impossible if returns could be represented by a normal distribution. In fact, given a normal distribution, a six-sigma event would occur once every many millions of years. If returns are distributed according to power laws,[31] however, events of this magnitude have a nonnegligible probability.

In discussing the fat tails of returns, it should be ascertained whether returns are fat tailed in the same way at every time horizon and whether financial crises can be considered instances of fat-tailed returns. An economic explanation of fat tails would also be necessary, along with an understanding of the economic implications of such a return distribution.

Are returns fat tailed in the same way at every time horizon?

As many academic studies have shown,[32] returns are fat tailed, and this fact is well known to practitioners. The nature of the tails, however, is not the same at every time horizon. Empirical testing has shown that stock returns at time horizons from minutes to a few days are fat tailed, whereas at time horizons of a month, the tails of returns are less fat. Of course, making this statement precise requires estimating the tails. At longer time horizons, it is more difficult to establish the exact statistical nature of stock returns because data are scarce. So, knowing whether yearly returns are fat tailed is difficult because the number of years for which reliable data are available is too small to estimate the tails confidently.

---

[31] A power law is a simple example of a fat-tailed distribution. Perhaps the best-known power law is Zipf's law, which states that the frequency of an outcome is inversely proportional to its ranking in a frequency table. Zipf's law applies to many phenomena from linguistics to economics. Pareto's law is the continuous distribution equivalent to Zipf's law.

[32] See, for example, Rachev, Menn, and Fabozzi (2005).

Other types of financial variables, such as corporate market capitalization, are pronouncedly fat tailed. Capitalization in particular appears to follow a power law. The magnitude of defaults by corporate bond issuers is also inherently fat tailed. Moving to derivatives, the magnitude of many events related to derivatives is inherently fat tailed.

Should market crashes be regarded as fat tails or as outliers?

Outliers are very large events separated from the bulk of the distribution, whereas a fat-tailed variable can assume any value. Again, this concept needs to be made more precise, but the intuition is clear. Johansen and Sornette (1998) suggested that large market crashes are outliers and not the fat tails of a distribution. The question is clearly difficult to answer given the rarity of these events.

Understanding the fat-tailed nature of returns and of large events, such as defaults, is a statistical task in principle and unrelated to any specific economic explanation. Predictions based on the fat-tailed distributions of returns are of a statistical nature. If it is known that some events have a fat-tailed distribution, very large events should be expected even if it is not known why they happen.

If we know empirically that returns are fat-tailed, we should expect possible large losses even if we do not know the economic mechanism that generates the losses. However, if we believe that crashes are outliers, we cannot adopt a purely statistical approach to estimating their likelihood but need to understand the eventual mechanism that generates the outlying events.

Much progress has been made recently in estimating tail events. In particular, extreme value theory (EVT), which is the theory that studies the distribution of extremes, is helpful in estimating fat-tailed phenomena. EVT is based on estimating only the tails. In this way, samples become smaller but distributions simplify. Progress has also been made in understanding the distribution of the extremes, in identifying new estimators, and in better defining the tail region through an understanding of the trade-offs implicit in estimating the tails.

What are the economic explanations of fat tails?

The explanation of fat tails is a major scientific effort not only in economics but also in many other disciplines, such as the theory of communications. In the field of economics, three basic explanations have been proposed. The first explanation is based on aggregation phenomena. It has been demonstrated that complex structures that include many elements subject to random interactions can develop aggregates whose magnitudes have fat-tailed distributions. Examples of aggregates include traders sharing mutual information and banks linked by derivative contracts. These notions have become particularly important with the growing complexity of financial markets, as we will explain later when we cover systemic risk.

A second type of explanation is based on self-reinforcing phenomena unrelated to aggregation. An example is momentum in stock prices, in which a price increase or decrease triggers additional price increases or decreases, thus creating large price movements over time.

The third explanation is based on the coupling of models—that is, by making the parameters of one model depend on another model. The best known of these coupled models are autoregressive conditional heteroscedasticity (ARCH) and generalized ARCH (GARCH), in which the volatility parameter of a linear model is determined by another autoregressive model. Other models include regime-shifting models. The coupling of models originates fat-tailed distributions—for example, mixture models in which each observation belongs to one of some number of different sources or categories that are randomly selected. Mixture models generate fat tails. Prolonged crises can be explained as the reversal of the direction of trends, and the mechanism that drives the direction of trends can be a separate model. The explanation of fat tails is important for practical reasons because it might help in identifying predictors of crises.

What are the economic implications of fat tails? Fat tails have many important economic implications. First, fat tails of returns or of default distributions can measure the likelihood of large losses. Therefore, the understanding of fat tails is a risk measurement tool in itself.

In addition, the fat tails of some economic variables can act as a trigger for other events. Understanding fat tails is important not only because of the losses generated directly but also because some fat-tailed events, although not critical in themselves, might start a cascade of negative phenomena. The financial markets witnessed one such phenomenon in the summer of 2007 when the reversal of specific trends, which could be regarded as an isolated event, forced investors to liquidate positions to cover margin calls. What was in itself a relatively marginal event rapidly turned into one of the most acute financial crises since the Great Depression.

In the presence of fat tails, the popular value at risk (VaR) measure is a poor measure of risk; rather, it is a confidence interval unable to discriminate between events (e.g., losses) slightly outside the confidence limits and those far outside. As mentioned in Chapter 2, many in asset management are now attentively looking at conditional VaR (CVaR) to mitigate this and other problems associated with VaR. CVaR is the expected value of losses that exceeds VaR. For example, the CVaR at 95 percent is the amount of expected losses in the highest 5 percent quantile. By definition, this expected loss exceeds VaR, and thus CVaR is a more conservative measure of risk. It should help communicate the risk inherent in fat-tailed distributions.

Risk and Factor Exposures

One lesson learned from the crisis seems to be the need for more economic understanding in risk management. Professor Schaefer remarked, "While the factors driving asset prices and their correlations may be quite well understood in normal times, in times of crisis, prices can move together in ways that they do not under usual circumstances. Getting a better handle on risk characteristics in times of crisis is both a hugely important task and a major challenge." In one sense, it might be said that the understanding of financial crises is the understanding of the hidden links in the economy. In commenting on how risk management can be improved, Professor Zhou noted, "Most of the existing (risk management) procedures seem data dependent. Qualitative links to and effects on the global economy might be explored."

Credit Risk, Counterparty Risk

The collapse of Lehman Brothers in September 2008 brought counterparty risk to the attention of investors who had been increasing their use of derivatives and structured products. Professor Schaefer commented, "I am a big believer in the potential of financial engineering to help manage risk, but long-term investors should think long and hard about whether, even ignoring the extra costs built into such products, they should be holding products that expose them to counterparty risk over the long term." It has become clear that counterparty risk is an instance of systemic risk. Counterparties that are sound in principle can become risky because of a web of interconnections. This connection raises the question of systemic risk.

Systemic Risk

We asked academics whether investors and the investment management industry should consider systemic risk. Professor Timmermann remarked, "We do need to pay attention to systemic risk given the future uncertainty about how effectively systemic risk can be handled and who will survive such events. For example, if a diversified pension fund sees all its assets plummet simultaneously, it will be underfunded and need to increase contributions or reduce benefits. This situation could lead to a liquidity crisis and ultimately the bankruptcy of the scheme. Systemic risk is important even though it doesn't occur very often."

Professor Berk agreed with the need to consider systemic risk:

If your job is to protect the value of your investments from adverse conditions, then you have to worry about those conditions. So, managers should always be worrying about systemic risk, now as well as in the past. Because such risk cannot be diversified away, investors demand a risk premium if they are exposed to it. There is no magic potion that can mitigate this kind of risk—somebody must hold this risk. Because crisis risk is endemic, it cannot be diversified away. To offload this kind of risk, you have to purchase insurance—that is, induce others to take the risk off your hands by paying them a risk premium.

Professor Ibbotson added, "Most risk is systemic risk. Most returns go up and down together. In 2008, everyone went down together; in 2009, everyone went up together. Xiong, Ibbotson, Idzorek, and Chen (2010) analyzed the variation of returns and found that about 70 percent of return variation is explained by the general market and the remainder is equally split between (1) the specific asset allocation and long-term policy and (2) implementation, including security selection, fees, and timing."

The possibility exists to turn systemic risk to one's advantage. Professor Zhou observed, "Keeping a blind eye does not help. Systemic risk does not arise overnight. It seems both possible and profitable to spot it."

Because the estimation of fat tails and the inversion of trends and correlations is such a delicate econometric task, it is important to find explanations for these phenomena that might enhance theoretical understanding. We discussed Minsky's (1986) analysis of economic systems, which established the link between the supply of credit and money and the formation of speculative bubbles. Although in the aftermath of the last financial crisis Minsky's analysis has enjoyed a renewal of interest, a full-fledged modeling effort based on his analysis of boom-and-bust cycles is still lacking. The recent massive injection of money into the economy by governments should make studying this phenomenon empirically feasible, given the data and computational power now available.

Another source of systemic risk, however, is attracting increasing attention from the academic community and governments; it is the complexity of the economic system composed of large and mutually interacting agents and the risk inherent in this complexity. In classical economic theory, rational economic agents do not interact; they are coordinated only by a price signal that is generated by the rational expectations of the agents themselves. In addition, in the classical model, each agent is too small to affect prices. Market crashes are difficult to explain within classical economic theory, but when economic systems are described as a set of mutually interacting agents, it becomes clear that powerful aggregation phenomena might be at work.

Aggregation phenomena can be described using the theories of percolation and of random graphs. Both theories deal with very large sets of units (e.g., economic agents) randomly connected through links. These randomly connected sets of units share an important feature; thresholds exist in the probability of random links beyond which significant change in the behavior of aggregates is induced. In particular, percolation[33] and random graphs exhibit a probability threshold below which the size of connected subsets follows an exponential distribution; at or above the threshold, the distribution becomes a power law distribution. Consequently,

---

[33] See Focardi and Fabozzi (2004) for an application of percolation theory to credit risk modeling.

giant components (or clusters) appear. The transition from small connected components to very large connected components that become the entire network is rapid and has the characteristics of a state transition. That is, below the threshold, the random network is formed of small isolated components, while at the threshold, giant components suddenly appear.

These ideas have potentially many applications in finance. Consider a set of traders or asset managers. They do not act in isolation but exchange information, often in an informal way. Traders exchanging information can be modeled as a set of mutually interacting agents because the exchange of information can trigger a change of opinion and, therefore, result in a modification of agents' trades. In general, clusters of agents who change opinion simultaneously are few and do not have a significant impact on markets. The theory of random structures, however, informs us that if the probability of interaction approaches a threshold, large networks can be formed. The probability of interaction can change because of external conditions that modify the propensity of traders to be influenced by others. For example, in moments of fear, traders are more prone to communicate and to be influenced by other traders' opinions.

It has been suggested that the fat tails of returns can be explained by agent aggregation, which creates a demand for some assets proportional to the size of connected components. As the distribution of the size of connected components is fat tailed, so are returns.[34]

Similar ideas regarding aggregation are now being proposed to model the risk of the financial system at large. Several authors have proposed to explicitly model the graph of relationships between financial institutions and to use results from network theory to model the risk inherent in networks. For example, Cont, Moussa, Minca, and Bastos (2009) proposed a Systemic Risk Index that includes economic factors affecting defaults as well as measures of the connectedness of networks. These ideas have come to the attention of financial authorities. In the United Kingdom, Andrew Haldane, executive director for Financial Stability at the Bank of England, suggested mapping the financial network topology and the introduction of regulations that affect the structure of networks.

Haldane (2009) observed that the theory of interconnected agents has been used successfully to model physical networks, such as the internet or power networks. Designers of internet browsers and other software are clearly interested in modeling the length of the path that links two sites. A milestone in these studies is Barabási and Albert (1999), who determined the distribution of the length of paths under realistic conditions. They concluded that the length of paths connecting sites

---

[34]See Cont and Bouchaud (2000).

follows a power law distribution, introducing a number of measures of the connectivity of a network. Haldane observed that models and measures developed in the context of communications might be applied to model the network of interbank relationships as a result of derivative contracts. He suggested that, to understand the level of financial risk, regulators adopt measures of network complexity.

The Squam Lake Working Group on Financial Regulation (2009)[35] has also put emphasis on the need to consider critical interactions between financial institutions. Noting that attempts by individual banks to remain solvent in a crisis can undermine the stability of the financial system as a whole, members of the working group argued in favor of a systemic regulator whose role should include gathering, analyzing, and reporting information about significant interactions and risks among financial institutions. These proposals are revolutionary. Thus far, regulators have put the focus on the management of a cushion of capital to protect against losses and less emphasis on modeling the network of relationships among financial institutions. It has become clear, however, that no reasonable amount of capital can protect against risks that originate from a highly interconnected financial structure.

Although the adoption of network concepts is currently proposed in the framework of regulatory actions, there is no *a priori* reason not to include these tools in the toolbox of risk managers. But given the difficulty in obtaining data, the updated mapping of financial networks might be challenging for asset managers and other financial institutions to obtain.

Can Macroeconomics Help?

Many sources, especially in continental Europe, remarked that macroeconomics will play a larger role in asset management in the future. We asked academics for their views about this statement. The academics we interviewed remarked that the timescales of finance and macroeconomics do not match. Some suggested that asset prices have more predictive power for the macroeconomy than the reverse. Professor Schaefer commented, "This view is exactly what one should expect because asset prices are forward looking and incorporate forecasts of future cash flows and, therefore, forecasts of the future state of the economy."

---

[35]Members of the group are Martin N. Baily (Brookings Institute), Andrew B. Bernard (Dartmouth College), John Y. Campbell (Harvard University), John H. Cochrane (University of Chicago), Douglas W. Diamond (University of Chicago), Darrell Duffie (Stanford University), Kenneth R. French (Dartmouth College), Anil K. Kashyap (University of Chicago), Frederic S. Mishkin (Columbia University), Raghuram G. Rajan (University of Chicago), David S. Scharfstein (Harvard University), Robert J. Shiller (Yale University), Hyun Song Shin (Princeton University), Matthew J. Slaughter (Dartmouth College), and René M. Stulz (Ohio State University).

New Risks As a Result of Complex Structured Products

As investors turn increasingly to complex structured products to enhance returns or to hedge against some risks, industry sources voiced concern about additional risks that these products might introduce. We asked academics what they thought. Professor Berk remarked, "This question is about cause and effect. The complicated financial products are a result of intense competition in financial markets. Although people used them to take on risk, they are not the underlying reason people took on the risk in the first place."

Professor Ibbotson added,

> The complexity of products has made it difficult for asset managers to rely on ratings. Rating agencies cannot understand the complexity of products. There are behavioral aspects. Given the competition and the need to perform, people are stretching for returns and are willing to take on more risk to get returns. Why stretch so hard to get returns in a low-return environment? Do we need to win at each moment? Do we have to be a winner even in a year in which returns are hard to get? Winning does not come cheap. You need sophisticated investors to understand this concept. Take Madoff: Investors were looking for someone who wins every time, but such consistency should be regarded with suspicion.

Professor Schaefer commented on the risk to investors in complex products:

> Often there is quite a serious problem. Some structured products are bought by people without the ability to fully evaluate their value; in other words, there is asymmetry of expertise. The risk of overpaying is high, and a long-term fund might be giving away many basis points in return without fully understanding it. Moreover, the bespoke nature of some products means that investors cannot rely on competition alone to ensure that they receive good value. Right now, there is even less competition than before as many banks are no longer able to participate in the market because of capital requirements (or have been taken over or simply disappeared). Competition in these markets is much less than perfect.

Underlining how complex products contributed to the past financial turmoil, Professor Zhu added,

> Because of the lack of transparency, asymmetry in information, and difficulties in valuing, risk-averse investors would dump and/or avoid those products when the first signal of trouble appears in the crisis. As Paul Krugman shows, the highly leveraged financial institutions have positively sloped demand curves. When markets go down, their demand for securities would go down with the market. The market could be stabilized if the demand for those securities from other investors would increase when prices are much lower. However, the complexity of the financial products prevents the stabilization factor from functioning, further exacerbating the crisis.

Future Advances

We have mentioned a number of advances in risk management that are now state-of-the-art from the academic point of view. These include the handling of fat-tailed distributions, extreme value theory, the handling of nonlinear correlations through copula functions, and new measures of risk, such as CVaR. These methodologies and measures will become part of risk management. It is also likely that some of the mathematical tools that we have for modeling networks and interconnectivity will be picked up by the industry, at least among those that should be concerned with systemic risk.

Another important trend will be the switch from static to dynamic techniques, which takes into account lagged values, thereby allowing for time-varying forecasts. The difficulty in using dynamic techniques is that, unlike static techniques, one can come up with forecasts but the forecasts may not be any good; forecasting is very difficult as financial markets are close to being efficient. As a result, dynamic techniques almost invariably extract a small amount of information from a large amount of noise. Many dynamic econometric methods are available, including factor models, scalar and vector autoregressive models, and regime-shifting models. In all these models, it is fundamental to use techniques that allow parsimonious representations, reducing the dimensionality of the model. Important new techniques for dimensionality reduction include random matrix theory as well as techniques to estimate the rank of matrices.

A better understanding of modeling high-frequency data will probably be needed. Presently, the modeling of trades at high frequency is still the preserve of a few financial institutions that have the techniques and the ability to access the market at a low cost. In trying to earn a small profit on a large number of trades, high-frequency trading is potentially disruptive to market operations. In practice, it is performed automatically by computer programs. This behavior creates new types of risk purely related to technology because it is possible that unforeseen interactions between programs, mistakes in the programs, or even deliberate action to confuse the market can disrupt market operations. Just as such physical systems' power grids implement sophisticated control systems to prevent power outages, the increasing diffusion of high-frequency trading might effectively require the introduction of controls to avoid a "market outage."

Protecting Investments in Future Crashes

We asked academics to identify likely candidates for future bubbles. It is fair to say that not many candidates were forthcoming, but among those mentioned are government bond prices, property prices in Southeast Asia, and emerging-markets assets. Professor Ibbotson does not believe that we are presently witnessing the formation of a new bubble but commented on the difficulty of staying out of the market when a bubble develops: "When you get into bubble periods, the tendency is to join the bubble and not get out. You need to be willing to take some relatively poor performance along the way because you can't tell when the bubble will pop." Investors be advised!

We also asked academics how investors might protect their assets from future bubbles. Professor Schaefer said, "The one lesson we should have learned from the recent market crash is the need to institutionalize the memory of the crisis. Irrational exuberance will no doubt return at some point, but we need to guard against it. Perhaps, especially in good times, investors should be made to attend seminars about financial history to remind them of the possibility of a crash." Concurring on the need to remind investors and asset managers alike that there really is a risk–return trade-off, Professor Finnerty noted, "We need to continue to promote investor understanding of the basic tenets of sound investing. If something looks too good to be true, it probably is! Behind those tempting juicy returns—high-yield bonds in the late 1980s, tech stocks in the late 1990s up to March 2000, and complex mortgage-backed products into early 2007—may be some potentially enormous hidden risks, which can completely wipe out the accumulated juicy returns if the investor disregards the risk–return trade-off and becomes complacent about investment risk."

Professor Ibbotson concurred that the problem is one of human behavior. Remarking that managing investment risk is in the realm of what we can do with mathematics, Professor Ibbotson said, "The problem is not the math but human behavior; people forget about the crisis and move on." He added some specific suggestions for investors: "(1) stay away from high leverage, (2) keep fees under control—fees can be high without outperformance, and (3) diversify investments."

References

Amenc, Noël, Philippe Malaise, and Lionel Martellini. 2004. "Revisiting Core–Satellite Investing: A Dynamic Model of Relative Risk Management." *Journal of Portfolio Management*, vol. 31, no. 1 (Fall):64–75.

Amenc, Noël, Philippe Malaise, Lionel Martellini, and Daphné Sfeir. 2003. "Tactical Style Allocation: A New Form of Market Neutral Strategy." *Journal of Alternative Investments*, vol. 6, no. 1 (Summer):8–22.

Ang, Andrew, William N. Goetzmann, and Stephen M. Schaefer. 2009. *Evaluation of Active Management of the Norwegian Government Pension Fund—Global.* Norwegian Ministry of Finance Report (14 December): www.regjeringen.no/en/dep/fin/Selected-topics/the-government-pension-fund/published-material-on-the-government-pen/reports-on-active-management-of-the-gove.html?id=588819.

Artzner, Philippe, Freddy Delbaen, Jean-Marc Eber, and David Heath. 1999. "Coherent Measures of Risk." *Mathematical Finance*, vol. 9, no. 3:203–228.

Association of Consulting Actuaries. 2009. *Statistical Analysis: 2009 Pension Trends Survey Results* (29 December).

Baker, Craig. 2008. "A Fairer Deal on Fees." Towers Watson (27 February).

Barabási, Albert-László, and Réka Albert. 1999. "Emergence of Scaling in Random Networks." *Science*, vol. 286, no. 5439 (15 October):509–512.

Bartram, Söhnke M., and Gordon M. Bodnar. 2009. "No Place to Hide: The Global Crisis in Equity Markets in 2008/2009." *Journal of International Money and Finance*, vol. 28, no. 8 (December):1246–1292.

Bernstein, Peter L. 2003. "Are Policy Portfolios Obsolete?" *Economics & Portfolio Strategy* newsletter (1 March). New York: Peter L. Bernstein, Inc.

Binder, Steffen, and Christian Nolterieke. 2009. "Insufficient Client Focus—A Survey of European Private Banks." European Private Banking Report, MyPrivateBanking.com (28 May): www.myprivatebanking.com.

Brinson, Gary P., Brian D. Singer, and Gilbert L. Beebower. 1991. "Determinants of Portfolio Performance II: An Update." *Financial Analysts Journal*, vol. 47, no. 3 (May/June):40–48.

©2010 The Research Foundation of CFA Institute

Campbell, Rachel A.J., Catherine S. Forbes, Kees G. Koedijk, and Paul Kofman. 2008. "Increasing Correlations or Just Fat Tails?" *Journal of Empirical Finance*, vol. 15, no. 2 (March):287–309.

Carhart, Mark M. 1997. "On Persistence in Mutual Fund Performance." *Journal of Finance*, vol. 52, no. 1 (March):57–82.

Carter, Drew. 2009. "U.K. Corporate Funds Add to Investment Staff." *Pensions & Investments* (30 November):30.

Comptroller of the Currency. 2005. *Collective Investment Funds: Comptroller's Handbook*. Washington, DC: U.S. Department of the Treasury.

Cont, Rama, and Jean-Philippe Bouchaud. 2000. "Herd Behavior and Aggregate Fluctuations in Financial Markets." *Macroeconomic Dynamics*, vol. 4, no. 2 (June):170–196.

Cont, Rama, Amal Moussa, Andreea Minca, and Edson Bastos. 2009. "Too Interconnected to Fail: Contagion and Systemic Risk in Financial Networks." Working paper, Columbia University.

EFAMA. 2009. "Worldwide Investment Fund Assets and Flows: Trends in the Second Quarter 2009." International Statistical Release, European Fund and Asset Management Association (29 October).

Embrechts, Paul, Claudia Klüppelberg, and Thomas Mikosch. 1997. *Modelling Extremal Events for Insurance and Finance*. New York: Springer-Verlag.

Ennis, Richard M. 2005. "Are Active Management Fees Too High?" *Financial Analysts Journal*, vol. 61, no. 5 (September/October):44–51.

———. 2009. "Parsimonious Asset Allocation." *Financial Analysts Journal*, vol. 65, no. 3 (May/June):6–10.

Fabozzi, Frank J., Francis Gupta, and Harry M. Markowitz. 2002. "The Legacy of Modern Portfolio Theory." *Journal of Investing*, vol. 11, no. 3 (Fall):7–22.

Fama, Eugene, and Kenneth French. 1992. "The Cross-Section of Expected Returns." *Journal of Finance*, vol. 47, no. 2 (June):427–465.

Focardi, Sergio M., and Frank J. Fabozzi. 2004. "A Percolation Approach to Modeling Credit Loss Distribution under Contagion." *Journal of Risk*, vol. 7, no. 1 (Fall):75–94.

———. 2009. "Black Swans and White Eagles: On Mathematics and Finance." *Mathematical Methods of Operations Research*, vol. 69, no. 3 (July):379–394.

Glover, Hannah. 2009. "Collective Investment Trusts Muscle in on DC Market." *Financial Times* (14 September):8.

Haldane, Andrew G. 2009. "Rethinking the Financial Network." Speech to the Financial Student Association in Amsterdam (28 April).

Hamilton, James D. 1989. "A New Approach to the Economic Analysis of Nonstationary Time Series and the Business Cycle." *Econometrica*, vol. 57, no. 2 (March):357–384.

Holden, Sarah, and Michael Hadley. 2009. "The Economics of Providing 401(k) Plans: Services, Fees, and Expenses, 2008." Investment Company Institute *Research Fundamentals*, vol. 18, no. 6 (August).

Ibbotson, Roger G., and Paul D. Kaplan. 2000. "Does Asset Allocation Policy Explain 40, 90, or 100 Percent of Performance?" *Financial Analysts Journal*, vol. 56, no. 1 (January/February):26–33.

Ibbotson, Roger G., Peng Chen, and Kevin X. Zhu. Forthcoming 2011. "ABCs of Hedge Funds: Alphas, Betas, and Costs." *Financial Analysts Journal*.

Ilmanen, Antti. 2003. "Stock Bond Correlation." *Journal of Fixed Income*, vol. 13, no. 2 (September):55–66.

Inker, Ben. 2008. "When Diversification Failed." GMO LLC. (December).

Investment Company Institute. 2009. *2009 Investment Company Fact Book.* 49th ed. Washington, DC: Investment Company Institute.

Investment & Pensions Europe. 2009a. "Jobs Go as AP1 Alters Asset Management Model." (11 February): www.ipe.com; retrieved 5 May 2010.

———. 2009b. "IPE European Institutional Asset Management Survey 2009." (July).

———. 2009c. "Fund Managers Return to Client Priorities." Investit Survey (7 August): www.ipe.com.

Jefferies & Company, Inc. 2007. "After the Belle Époque: The Future of Fund Management." White paper (December).

Johansen, Anders, and Didier Sornette. 1998. "Stock Market Crashes Are Outliers." *European Physical Journal B*, vol. 1, no. 2 (February):141–143.

Johnson Associates, Inc. 2009. "Financial Services Compensation: Third Quarter Trends and Year-End Projections" (5 November).

Kanas, Angelos, and Georgios P. Kouretas. 2005. "A Cointegration Approach to the Lead-Lag Effect among Size-Sorted Equity Portfolios." *International Review of Economics & Finance*, vol. 14, no. 2:181–201.

Lo, Andrew W., and A. Craig MacKinlay. 1990. "When Are Contrarian Profits Due to Stock Market Overreaction?" *Review of Financial Studies*, vol. 3, no. 2 (Summer):175–205.

Longin, François, and Bruno Solnik. 2001. "Extreme Correlation of International Equity Markets." *Journal of Finance*, vol. 56, no. 2 (April):649–676.

Mannion, Graham, and Nigel Peaple. 2009. "DC Default Funds: Today & Tomorrow." National Association of Pension Funds and PensionDCisions (October).

Maslakovic, Marko. 2009. "Fund Management 2009." Research report, International Financial Services, London (October).

McKinsey & Company. 2006. *The Asset Management Industry in 2010*. New York: McKinsey & Company.

———. 2009a. *Asset Management Survey 2009*. New York: McKinsey & Company.

———. 2009b. *Recovering from the Storm: The New Economic Reality for U.S. Asset Managers*. New York: McKinsey & Company.

Mercer. 2009. *Shedding Light on Responsible Investment: Approaches, Returns and Impact*. New York: Mercer LLC.

Mercer and United Nations Environment Programme Finance Initiative. 2007. *Demystifying Responsible Investment Performance*. Toronto: Mercer LLC.

Merton, Robert C. 1971. "Optimal Consumption and Portfolio Rules in a Continuous-Time Model." *Journal of Economic Theory*, vol. 3, no. 4 (December): 373–413.

———. 1980. "On Estimating the Expected Return on the Market: An Exploratory Investigation." *Journal of Financial Economics*, vol. 8, no. 4 (December): 323–361.

Minsky, Hyman P. 1982. *Can "It" Happen Again?: Essays on Instability and Finance*. Armonk, NY: M.E. Sharpe.

———. 1986. *Stabilizing an Unstable Economy*. 1st ed. New Haven, CT: Yale University Press.

Nolterieke, Christian. 2009. "Cut the Costs of Wealth Management." (www.myprivatebanking.com; retrieved 5 May 2010).

Nuttall, Jennifer A., and John Nuttall. 1998. "Asset Allocation Claims—Truth or Fiction?" Working paper.

Nuttall, John. 2000. "'Does Asset Allocation Policy Explain 40, 90, or 100 Percent of Performance?': Comments." *Financial Analysts Journal*, vol. 56, no. 3 (May/June):16.

"Off the Record: Decisions, Decisions." 2009. *IPE Magazine* (December).

Plerou, Vasiliki, Parameswaran Gopikrishnan, Bernd Rosenow, Luís A. Nunes Amaral, Thomas Guhr, and H. Eugene Stanley. 2002. "Random Matrix Approach to Cross Correlations in Financial Data." *Physical Review E: Statistical, Nonlinear, and Soft Matter Physics*, vol. 65, no. 6 (June):066126.

Rachev, Svetlozar T., and Stefan Mittnik. 2000. *Stable Paretian Models in Finance*. Hoboken, NJ: John Wiley & Sons.

Rachev, Svetlozar T., Christian Menn, and Frank J. Fabozzi. 2005. *Fat-Tailed and Skewed Asset Return Distributions: Implications for Risk Management, Portfolio Selection, and Option Pricing*. Hoboken, NJ: John Wiley & Sons.

Reinhart, Carmen M., and Kenneth S. Rogoff. 2008. "This Time Is Different: A Panoramic View of Eight Centuries of Financial Crises." NBER Working Paper No. 13882 (March).

Rockafellar, R. Tyrrell, and Stanislav Uryasev. 2000. "Optimization of Conditional Value-at-Risk." *Journal of Risk*, vol. 2, no. 3 (Spring):21–41.

Ross, Stephen. 1976. "The Arbitrage Theory of Capital Asset Pricing." *Journal of Economic Theory*, vol. 13, no. 3 (December):341–360.

Russell Reynolds Associates. 2009. "Defining the New Reality for the Asset and Wealth Management Industry. Recruiting and Compensation Trends." Russell Reynolds Associates, Inc.

SEI Knowledge Partnership. 2008. *Collective Investment Trusts: The New Wave in Retirement Investing*. Oaks, PA: SEI Investments Developments, Inc.

Sharpe, William F. 1964. "Capital Asset Prices: A Theory of Market Equilibrium under Conditions of Risk." *Journal of Finance*, vol. 19, no. 3 (September):425–442.

———. 1992. "Asset Allocation: Management Styles and Performance Measurement." *Journal of Portfolio Management*, vol. 18, no. 2 (Winter):7–19.

Shiller, Robert J. 2006. "Life-Cycle Portfolios as Government Policy." Cowles Foundation Paper 1182 (www.econ.yale.edu/~shiller/pubs/p1182.pdf; retrieved 5 May 2010).

Squam Lake Working Group on Financial Regulation. 2009. "A Systemic Regulator for Financial Markets." Working paper (May): www.squamlakegroup.org; retrieved 5 May 2010.

Taleb, Nassim. 2007. *The Black Swan: The Impact of the Highly Improbable.* New York: Random House.

Tonello, Matteo, and Stephan Rabimov. 2009. *The 2009 Institutional Investment Report: Trends in Asset Allocation and Portfolio Composition.* Report No. 1455-09-RR, The Conference Board (October).

Towers Watson. 2008. *Defining Moments: The Pensions and Investment Industry of the Future.* New York: Towers Watson.

———. 2009. *2009 Global Pension Assets Study.* New York: Towers Watson.

van Nunen, Anton. 2007. *Fiduciary Management: Blueprint for Pension Fund Excellence.* Hoboken, NJ: John Wiley & Sons.

Xiong, James, Roger G. Ibbotson, Thomas Idzorek, and Peng Chen. 2010. "The Equal Importance of Asset Allocation and Active Management." *Financial Analysts Journal*, vol. 66, no. 2 (March/April):22–30.

Ziemba, William T. 2003. *The Stochastic Programming Approach to Asset, Liability, and Wealth Management.* Charlottesville, VA: Research Foundation of CFA Institute.